COLLECTED POEMS

Also by Michael Donaghy

Dances Learned Last Night:
Poems 1975–1995

Conjure

Safest

The Shape of the Dance

MICHAEL DONAGHY

COLLECTED POEMS

PICADOR

First published 2009 by Picador
an imprint of Pan Macmillan, a divsion of Macmillan Publishers Limited
Pan Macmillan, 20 New Wharf Road, London N1 9RR
Basingstoke and Oxford
Associated companies throughout the world
www.panmacmillan.com

ISBN 978-0-330-45629-6

Shibboleth originally published 1988 by Oxford University Press,
including 'Slivers' and 'Reader' and a different version of 'Letter'.
Errata originally published 1993 by Oxford University Press.
Conjure first published 2000 by Picador
Safest first published 2005 by Picador

Printed in the UK by CPI Antony Rowe, Chippenham, Wiltshire

Visit **www.picador.com** to read more about all our books
and to buy them. You will also find features, author interviews and
news of any author events, and you can sign up for e-newsletters
so that you're always first to hear about our new releases.

Contents

Introduction

(on Michael Donaghy:
Black Ice, Rain and the City of God)

Michael Donaghy (1954–2004) was a fastidious poet, slow to write and slow to publish. He was always prepared to endure the frustration of sitting out the time it took for a poem to begin to emerge in order to have the equally frustrating pleasure of working on it. He once claimed, more or less jokingly, to write only three poems a year. This *Collected Poems* contains roughly a hundred and fifty, of which about a third were unpublished at his death in September 2004 at the age of fifty.

This is not a large corpus, but it is remarkably diverse and exciting, and one turns repeatedly in sorrow and anger to the fact that he was not able to complete his work. W. H. Auden proposed that poets die when their work is finished: Donaghy is clearly an exception. The 'late' material in *Safest*, and some of the uncollected pieces here, indicate that a further stage of development was in progress, albeit inescapably shadowed by the intensifying awareness of mortality which he experienced after his health grew fragile in the last few years of his life. A number of the poems strike a valedictory note, but Donaghy the poet had by no means exhausted his art, and there are signs that he was moving towards the further reconciliation of his wit and learning with greater lyrical economy and directness.

Wit and learning were among the powerful attractions of Donaghy's first collection, *Shibboleth* (1988). He didn't simply have opinions: he *knew* things – about literature, history, music, science, anthropology, non-Western cultures. The book boldly announced his arrival among other poets of his generation, including Jo Shapcott and Matthew Sweeney. Donaghy was doing something different again from either of these strongly contrasting poets. In his constellation of interests and his delight in the connectedness of things, he most resembles his exact contemporary Ian Duhig, like him a poet of Irish descent.

For those who cared to notice, Donaghy was among other things renovating some features of the scholarly, formalist American poetry of the 1950s and 60s, whose leading exponents were Richard Wilbur, Anthony Hecht and James Merrill. By the 1980s these poets had little readership, especially among the young, on this side of the Atlantic, because they had been eclipsed by (according to taste) Lowell and Plath, the Beats and the New York Poets. What Donaghy shared with Wilbur in particular was a love of the art, and artfulness, on its own account, as a sign of imaginative plenitude. Those who enjoyed poems of Wilbur's such as 'Shame' and 'The Undead' and 'The Mind-Reader' could recognize a kindred spirit in Donaghy, one free of the gentility to which Wilbur was sometimes prone. Equally, those who admired Hecht's 'More Light! More Light!' or 'The Dover Bitch' saw what Donaghy was about while noting the absence of that faint superior coldness which can seem to impede Hecht's work. An Irish working-class upbringing in an ethnically diverse and at times dangerous district of the Bronx gave Donaghy's work a salty vernacular life which in turn lent his forms their packed, excited urgency. And the poems are often talking *to* someone – a lover, a ghost, the passer-by drawn in to hear the story. This sense of address to the reader recalls Frost, while the simultaneous aspiration to visionary grandeur reveals among other things the depth of Donaghy's immersion in Yeats.

Such a list risks creating the image of an imaginary monster, the Donaghy – something described but never actually seen or heard. Donaghy was of course far more than the sum of his reading. He was of the academy (until he couldn't stand it and gave up his graduate studies: he had contemptuously funny things to say about the orthodoxies of theory), but he was not an academic poet. The masters in his pantheon shone with special intensity because their presence proved that art, rather than attitude, or ownership, was at the core of his interests.

> . . . It's something that we've always known:
> Though we command the language of desire,
> The voice of ecstasy is not our own.
> We long to lose ourselves amid the choir
> Of the salmon twilight and the mackerel sky,
> The very air we take into our lungs,
> And the rhododendron's cry.

Paradox is fundamental to Donaghy's imagination, and the impassioned and hilarious 'Pentecost', an early poem about the cries of lovers, is one of his boldest examples. Language is deployed to evoke a state beyond itself – speaking in tongues, which crosses the division between the self and the world. In effect, consciousness is brought to serve its own renunciation, at the merging of the sacred and profane. Where Marvell's 'green thought in a green shade' is the apotheosis of solitude, this poem imagines an addressee:

> And when you lick the sweat along my thigh,
> Dearest, we renew the gift of tongues.

It would be a mistake to read these closing lines as a glib or cavalier QED. They offer a joke, issue a challenge, invite the partner to engage in a lovers' amused conspiracy, and they also pretend to test the partner's credulity for the purposes of a seduction which has already been accomplished. The amusement is not directed at but enjoyed with the lover. The harmonic range of tones is very rich, the voice made present to us as to the object of desire, a method indebted to Browning but clearly renewed by Donaghy.

'Pentecost' begins with the neighbours furiously hammering on the bedroom walls – to which the ultimate riposte is a religious-philosophical defence of selfishness. Its most prominent source is Donne's 'The Good Morrow' – though of course Donne's transcendent self-assurance is quite different from Donaghy's proposed shedding of identity. As with many another poet, identity, time and memory are fundamental terms of Donaghy's imagination. While they are 'traditional', they figure in Donaghy's work not as tropes securely anchoring him to an unthreatening past but as provocative crises in which the imagination engages anew with its inheritance.

We might say that Donaghy's ultimate subject was human nature, the question being of what that nature consisted. The poems are full of assumed, discarded, temporary selves (see 'Smith', 'Shibboleth' and 'Ramon Fernandez?' among the early work), creations necessary for legitimacy, survival, change of allegiance. They are not the self-creations of existentialism, still less of banal scientism, since they acknowledge the corridors of religion, history and culture down which the speakers have been led to the poems' eventual declarations. For Donaghy's characters there is no way out of the labyrinth; for the unbelieving poet the language and imagery of belief are not discredited fetishes to be discarded by atheistic maturity, but crucial means of

vision and understanding. 'City of God' from *Errata* (1993) tells of a
failed priest returning to the Bronx from the seminary, obsessed with
practising a form of memory art:

> He needed a perfect cathedral in his head,
> he'd whisper, so that by careful scrutiny
> the mind inside the cathedral inside the mind
> could find the secret order of the world
> and remember every drop on every face
> in every summer thunderstorm.

The teller offers us both the poignant absurdity of this project
and the reverence in which it is conceived. In the kind of joke that
Donaghy enjoyed, the deranged psycho-encyclopaedist is indepen-
dently covering the same ground as Borges's Funes the Memorious, as
well as recalling the 'authentic' but uncategorizable labours of Pierre
Menard in writing *Don Quixote* in a form identical to but wholly
independent of Cervantes'. More problematically, the character in
'City of God' seems to be committing a supreme heresy, even in the
attempt to glorify the Creator, by undertaking to comprehend and
encompass and thus internally reproduce His works. The poem closes
as narrator and madman contemplate 'a storefront voodoo church
beneath the el | . . . | its window strange with plaster saints and
seashells' – signs of faith, of pilgrimage, and of the ungovernable
character of the religious imagination.

It has been suggested that Donaghy's status might suffer from his
lack of interest in politics, but in fact *Shibboleth* contains a number
of poems, adjacently placed, whose material is inescapably political
– 'Auto da Fé', 'Ramon Fernandez?', 'Partisans' (which mirrors
'Shibboleth') and 'Majority'. This bleak series that progresses through
the attempt to understand the appeal of Franco's cause, the nature
of allegiance, the banality of political terror, and lastly the horrors of
complacent ignorance as (it would seem) embodied in the attitudes
of the 'majority' of Donaghy's fellow Americans. ('The Safe House',
from *Safest*, poignantly recounts the imaginary future of American
leftists who shared an apartment with a concealed copy of the revo-
lutionary *Manual of the Weather Underground*.) Throughout these
poems, the inseparability of religion and politics presents itself in
various ways. 'Auto da Fé', a sonnet with an intriguing ballad-like feel,

as though half-meant for singing, tells of an uncle who fought with the Irish volunteers in the Fascist cause in the Spanish Civil War (1936–39). In the poem's dream-encounter, the speakers debate this allegiance. Goya's *The Sleep of Reason* is cited without attributing the reference to either of the participants (the Church always claims the monopoly of Reason) and the poem moves on from discourse to image:

> The shape his hand made sheltering the flame
> Was itself a kind of understanding.
> But it would never help me to explain
> Why my uncle went to fight for Spain,
> For Christ, for the Caudillo, for the King.

'Yet man is born into trouble, as the sparks fly upward', declares Job 5: 7, and the next verse continues: 'I would seek unto God, and unto God would I commit my cause'. The image of the lit match invokes both a Catholic Hell and the obligation of the faithful to protect Holy Mother Church and the inferno which burns encouragingly at the base of her theology. (There is an entire essay to be written about the role of fire in Donaghy's work.) In the Holy Trinity named in the last line, the uncle's commitment seems to entail seeing 'the caudillo', Franco, as a grim practical embodiment of the working of the Holy Spirit – an act requiring a subjugation of the self unthinkable to a poet such as Donaghy, who remarked that he himself had a lifelong problem with authority, as anyone who tried to get him to meet a deadline or catch a train could testify.

'Ramon Fernandez?' is an altogether more complicated piece of work. Any reader of modern poetry will know Wallace Stevens' 'The Idea of Order at Key West', written in 1934 and published in his collection *Ideas of Order* (1936). Towards the close of the poem, the speaker asks 'Ramon Fernandez' to explain why the lights of the vessels in the harbour seem to impose an order on the darkened sea. This rhetorical question enables Stevens to go on and reorganize its materials as a statement of the 'maker's' 'blessed rage' for order, rather than undertake an answer which would either be impossible or tautologous. In his study *Wallace Stevens: A Literary Life*, Tony Sharpe explains that following the publication of *Ideas of Order*, Stevens was concerned to formulate a response to the Marxist critic Stanley Burnshaw, who saw him as the poetic representative of a doomed, privileged class soon to be swept aside. In a letter Stevens declared himself, rather implausibly, to be of the Left, by which he may really have meant that while (like several major modernist poets) he had felt the aesthetic allure of Reaction, he was not a Fascist.

Ramon Fernandez was an invention for the purposes of the poem – a non-speaking companion. The name is by no means unusual, and Stevens declared that he did not intend to refer to anyone in particular, although he acknowledged that he had heard of the French critic Ramon Fernandez, a contributor, like Stevens, to the magazine the *Dial*. In the period 1934–37 the actual Fernandez moved from anti-Fascism to membership of the Fascist Parti Populaire Français led by the ex-Communist Jacques Doriot, in bitter opposition to the Popular Front government of Leon Blum. Both Doriot and Fernandez became eager collaborators following the fall of France in 1940. Donaghy's poem is 'about' neither the historical Ramon Fernandez, nor Stevens' 'Ramon Fernandez', but both identities are present in the wings, as are Stevens' 1937 poem 'The Man with the Blue Guitar' (from the 1937 collection of the same name) and, presumptively, Picasso's 1903 Blue Period painting *The Old Guitarist*, which was exhibited in Stevens' home town of Hartford, Connecticut in 1934 (also the year when 'The Idea of Order at Key West' was written). It was of course Picasso who delivered one of the most memorable – and artistically uncompromised – responses to the atrocity of the Civil War, in his painting *Guernica* (1937). Among the famous facts about Stevens is that despite his taste for the exotic and his extensive imaginative travels, he never visited Europe, but in Donaghy's poem much that, explicitly or otherwise, concerns Stevens is transported to the Fascist siege of Barcelona, to the sphere of practicality and survival.

This fairly complex background suggests the richness of the resources Donaghy could bring to a poem, as well as the double vision he offers in this one. The reader too is likely to bring some literary-cultural knowledge to a poem which also has its own story to tell. That story underwrites the urgent, inescapable relevance of the artistic questions Stevens raises, by showing that in the age of totalitarianism nothing lies outside or above the sphere of the political.

A hero to the Republican troops who sing his songs when going off to battle in the Fascist invasion of Catalonia in January 1939, Fernandez is also a composer of choice for the forces of Franco, with

'A few words changed, not many.' Eventually 'he vanished back across the front', perhaps to suggest that an audience is an audience whatever its political stripe, perhaps that it was the border rather than the musician that moved. In the meantime, the Lenin Barracks clock, beneath which he played at noon, its hands arrested at half-past eleven, is struck by a stray round and the hands are blown off, leaving 'the face | To glare like a phase of the moon across the burning city.' The background presence of another reactionary poet, W. B. Yeats, can be felt here. In 'The Phases of the Moon' from *The Wild Swans at Coole* (1919), Michael Robartes summarizes the moon's twenty-eight phases, noting that 'there's no human life at the full or the dark' – for example, at the dark noon of the Fascist triumph, which was assisted by members of Eoin O'Duffy's blueshirts serving among the Volunteer Brigade, like the uncle in 'Auto da Fé' – blueshirts for whom Yeats had at one point written marching songs (though these were apparently too verbose for the purpose).

Donaghy was more aware than most of the ultimate sterility of the poem-as-anecdote which is so heavily represented on the contemporary scene. As 'Ramon Fernandez?' and many other poems demonstrate, his search was always for a deeper, more extended resonance than that offered by mere sentimental recognition. At the same time, his range of learning was present in the texture of his poems rather than appearing as a prohibition to those less well informed than himself. His work avoids the not uncommon tendency to confuse erudition itself with poetry. One of the reasons he liked living in the UK was that the reading and listening audience for poetry which seemed to him to have gone missing in the United States was still to be found here, and the most complex of his poems will always extend the courtesy of an invitation rather than an admonition or a dressing-down.

Donaghy's most extended piece of critical writing, *Wallflowers*, begins by observing a crowd of dancers at a ceilidh – the local dance being perhaps the most democratic of the arts – and derives its discussion of pattern and memorability from the scuff-marks left on the floor by the dancers' feet. He was always keen to affirm the highest artistic standards while insisting that poetry must live in the wide community of its readers and listeners, and his own public readings were delivered from memory, like the traditional Irish music in which he also excelled as a flute player. Some of his most memorable poems concern music –

the haunting 'The Tuning', for example, or 'Remembering Steps to Dances Learned Last Night' (the latter taking place after the returning Ulysses' massacre of Penelope's suitors) – and the sequence 'O'Ryan's Belt', from *Errata* (1993), was central to his work. It seems, too, from the previously unpublished material included here, that although he had published this sequence he had by no means finished with it. The triangular relationship of artist and material and audience is part of these half a dozen poems as it is of 'Ramon Fernandez?', and surmounting everything is the idea of what Pound called 'a live tradition', in this case sustained by memory and personal transmission, the common property of those who care for it.

Donaghy was neither pious nor sentimental on this topic. The story which perhaps most interested him is told in 'A Reprieve', where the Chicago Police Chief Francis O'Neill offers the fiddler Nolan, who has probably killed a Chinese man in a fight, the chance to leave town on a freight train if he plays his music so that O'Neill can transcribe it. For this night O'Neill has a Medici's powers of life and death and patronage, while Nolan's art receives official sanction – the further sting being that Nolan must try against nature and tradition to play the jigs the same way twice in order that they can be recorded on paper, and thus, in a sense, betrayed. The knowledge that the true art is inseparable from everyday contingency and circumstance is given a humorous airing elsewhere, in 'The Natural and Social Sciences' from *Shibboleth*, where a visiting American asks a player what the last tune was and is told, 'Ask my father', which he takes for an answer rather than an instruction.

Vanishing, escaping, illusory, unavailable for consultation, many of the characters in Donaghy's crowded yet often solitary world seem to reflect his own sense of exile. He was from the working class but educated out of it, a scholar who gave up the academy, a leading poet in Britain whose work was little known in the country where he grew up. He recalled that he injured his parents by insisting that he was an American rather than, as they believed, an Irish boy who happened to be living in New York, while the last twenty-odd years of his life were spent in England with only occasional visits to the United States to give readings. To many people of Irish extraction this is a version of a familiar story, part of the complex and continuing diaspora that can lead anywhere except 'home' and that can make questions of 'where your people were from' of interest mainly to the enquirer. Many of its features held no interest for Donaghy, but the theme of connection and disconnection, separation and reconciliation, was an abiding one, and it emerged most clearly in his last completed book, his third collection, *Conjure* (2000). The book opens with a series of three poems dealing with near misses and attempted encounters with fathers. The poems share a certain hermeticism in that while the author's 'actual circumstances' (he spoke at times of his father) are somewhere in the offing, the poems take place in an apparently fictionalized context and are all in some way concerned with lies and illusions and attempts to invoke what is not there. The book's title, with its imperative form – *Conjure* – leads back to the history of that word, which takes in senses including plot, conspire, swear an oath, bind together, call upon, appeal to a sacred person or thing, implore, invoke, charm, bewitch, employ magic. This etymology combines the sacred with the profane, illusion with ultimate reality, faith with deception, self with self-invention:

> 'My father's sudden death has shocked us all'
> Even me, and I've just made it up'.
> 'The Excuse'

> Do I stand here not knowing the words
> when someone walks in?
> 'Not Knowing the Words'

> This isn't easy. I've only half the spell,
> and I won't be born for twenty years.
> 'Caliban's Books'

The speaker cannot *know* the father, though he may well turn into him. This is an inheritance he is powerless to evade, and its responsibilities are most strongly felt when the child becomes, literally, the father. In the book's closing poem, the Coleridgean 'Haunts', dedicated to Donaghy's son Ruairi, the child himself comforts the father by simply existing, able to dispel the fears attendant on the adult night. In a sense, the child frees the man of the question of himself: *pass it on*, as the saying goes.

In a more sombre sense, transmission is also a significant part of 'Black Ice and Rain', perhaps the most brilliant poem among many fine pieces in *Conjure*. It is the story of a not-quite ménage à trois involving the narrator and a young couple he meets at a party, told retrospectively to a young woman he has followed into her bedroom at another party some time later. The pretext for his narration is that he can see that he and his listener have important things in common. One is, apparently, an unusual sensitivity (something missing in the boring party they have deserted, a party on which the speaker at any rate is dependent for enabling him to draw this perhaps adolescent distinction). Another is a sense of destiny so elaborate as to encompass the actions of chance. A third is the susceptibility to the pull of memory: 'the past falls open anywhere.'

The poem recalls Eliot's 'Portrait of a Lady', with the male and female roles reversed, retaining a sense of sterile erotic futility and manipulation. More than that, it offers the complex riches of a story by Henry James, where an apparently cultured society is stalked by cruelty and perversity and we witness the indulgence of a power whose near-intangibility serves to enhance its effect. In 'Black Ice and Rain' the speaker's confession is an act of cruelty towards the listener, whatever moral awareness it shows from line to line. In an earlier time the listener might at least have reasonably complained that she and the speaker had not been introduced, but now, in a period of insistent informality, the 'truth' is held to be its own social justification, and this predator of the mind is at liberty to pass on his own torments. The poem is full of shifting depths, and each repeated reading finds it renewed, but one of the most significant features is the balance between the religious background, mocked and discredited by the young couple as they endlessly sketch quote-marks on the air, and the apparent meaninglessness of the suffering that chance has inflicted on the object of the narrator's former desire by the car accident which has killed her partner. She may have got religion finally, but her grief empties into a void. Worse (for the narrator), not only have her looks been destroyed, but now that he could have her to himself it is clear that it was her unavailability that made her attractive.

> Then, having lain at last all night beside her,
> having searched at last that black-walled room,
> the last unopened chamber of my heart,
> and found there neither pity nor desire

but an assortment of religious kitsch,
I inched my arm from under her and left.

The narration, we remember, is staged in a bedroom at a party, while the rhetoric manages to be both stagey enough for a proscenium theatre and compellingly intimate its disclosure; both melodramatic and self-mocking; and unable or unwilling to credit the original integrity of any of its 'material'. Its fascinated (and rapturously self-fascinated) coldness recalls a major character from another novelist, the composer Adrian Leverkuhn from Thomas Mann's *Doktor Faustus*, who sold his soul to the Devil in order to be able to make music that could escape the confines of late romanticism. The result was marked by brutal parodies of feelings it had allegedly outgrown. With the characters of 'Black Ice and Rain' we are far from high art as practised in early twentieth-century Munich, but though the characters have no art of their own to make, only attitudes to strike, the human stakes are the same, and while the narrator makes a performance of his damnation, its psychic reality is not to be denied.

I've discussed 'Black Ice and Rain' in novelistic terms, through story, plot and character, in order to indicate Donaghy's artistic confidence. He's not simply rubbing up against fiction in the familiar timid and affectionate manner of a great many poets. He incorporates its forms and possibilities into the work while retaining the pacing, orchestration and variety of register which are the province of a poem. The poem more than stands its ground. What we have in 'Black Ice and Rain' is much more than another honourable addition to the genre of dramatic monologue. The poem offers a compelling renewal of the genre's possibilities, applied to subjects – belief, value, the confusion of art with the self and the self with the good – which the era of post-modernity has lent new colours and new urgency. The poem is also, slyly, circumstantially, damningly, a critique of postmodernity as a mass cultural movement/product on the grounds of its simultaneous fetishization of 'creativity' and denial of artistic authenticity. Donaghy disapproved of the notion of artistic 'progress', with its banal suggestion that 'now' is somehow better than 'then'; he would even have disputed the notion that at bottom 'now' is even *different* from then. For him – as it surely should be for us – the poetry that matters, that deserves to live, that engages the imagination and nourishes the memory, emerges in contact with 'a live tradition'. It offers itself to a general audience as both challenge and invitation, to create a space which can be colonized neither by vulgarity nor remote self-regard. It is, in the teeth of the odds, poetry undertaken as an act of good faith.

SEAN O'BRIEN
Newcastle
October 2008

SHIBBOLETH

Contents

Machines

Dearest, note how these two are alike:
This harpsichord pavane by Purcell
And the racer's twelve-speed bike.

The machinery of grace is always simple.
This chrome trapezoid, one wheel connected
To another of concentric gears,
Which Ptolemy dreamt of and Schwinn perfected,
Is gone. The cyclist, not the cycle, steers.
And in the playing, Purcell's chords are played away.

So this talk, or touch if I were there,
Should work its effortless gadgetry of love,
Like Dante's heaven, and melt into the air.

If it doesn't, of course, I've fallen. So much is chance,
So much agility, desire, and feverish care,
As bicyclists and harpsichordists prove

Who only by moving can balance,
Only by balancing move.

Pentecost

The neighbours hammered on the walls all night,
Outraged by the noise we made in bed.
Still we kept it up until by first light
We'd said everything that could be said.

Undaunted, we began to mewl and roar
As if desire had stripped itself of words.
Remember when we made those sounds before?
When we built a tower heavenwards
They were our reward for blasphemy.
And then again, two thousand years ago,
We huddled in a room in Galilee
Speaking languages we didn't know,
While amethyst uraeuses of flame
Hissed above us. We recalled the tower
And the tongues. We knew this was the same,
But love had turned the curse into a power.

See? It's something that we've always known:
Though we command the language of desire,
The voice of ecstasy is not our own.
We long to lose ourselves amid the choir
Of the salmon twilight and the mackerel sky,
The very air we take into our lungs,
And the rhododendron's cry.

And when you lick the sweat along my thigh,
Dearest, we renew the gift of tongues.

A Miracle

This will never do. Get the bird
Of gold enamelling out of the den.
I'm *reading*. Gin, white as winter sun,
Is blending juniper with oxygen.

Divinity is imminent. In the parlour
The crystal tinkling into words
Announces the arrival, through the mirror,
Of the host of stars and hummingbirds.

The angels have come early for the miracle.
They've gotten into the bar and drunk it dry.
Grinning, staggering, shedding feathers,
They can barely stand up, let alone fly.

One armoured, peacock-feathered cherub
Holds my copy of the future to the glass
And reads backwards (as they do in heaven)
Of how this evening will come to pass.

The seraphim are fencing on the lawn.
Thrust and parry, tipsy physical chess.
'The Conversation of the Blades', they call it,
The actual clink and whirr, the holiness.

Analysand

(Judges 12: 5–6)

I've had an important dream. But that can wait.
I want to talk about Ephraim Herrero
And the cobalt-blue tattoo of Mexico
That graced his arm above the wrist.

We were his disciples back in school.
The hours I spent echoing his accent,
Facing off to the mirror, smoothing my jacket
Over the bulge of a kitchen knife . . .

Once he held a razor to my throat . . .
But we've been over that a hundred times.
Did I tell you he won the Latin prize?
So you see it was more than contempt and fear

That drew us to him. The day that he got done
For selling envelopes of snow in May
Behind Our Lady of Guadaloupe
We were as much relieved as lost.

When the day of judgement came we were in court
Backing the loser, the soul of perjury
Wearing a tie he must have stolen from me
And someone else's Sunday suit.

It was a kick to see him so afraid.
And when he took the stand and raised his hand,
And his sleeve went south of the Rio Grande
I saw at once which side I was on.

Which brings me to the dream, if we have time.
I'm wading across a freezing river at night
Dressed in that suit and tie. A searchlight
Catches me mid-stream. I try to speak.

But someone steps between me and the beam.
The stars come out as if for an eclipse.
Slowly he raises his finger to his lips.
I wake before he makes that tearing sound.

More Machines

The clock of love? A smallish, round affair
That fits in the palm. A handy prop
Like any of these: compare
The pebble, the pearl, and the water drop.
They're all well made. But only one will prove
A fitting timepiece for our love.

To the pebble, the sun is a meteor,
The days a strobe, the years are swift.
Its machinery moves imperceptibly
Like the stars and continental drift.
But it's not for timing human love – it never *stops*.
Let us consider then the water drop

As it falls from the spigot during a summer storm
A distance of three feet. What does it see?
The lightning etched forever on the hot slate sky,
The birds fixed in an eternal V . . .
It falls so fast it knows no growth or changes.
A quick dog-fuck is all it measures

And it serves the beast as the stone serves God.
But our love doesn't hold with natural law.
Accept this small glass planet then, a shard
Grown smooth inside an oyster's craw.
Like us, it learns to opalesce
In darkness, in cold depths, in timelessness.

Deceit

The slate grey cloud comes up too fast.
The cornfield whispers like a fire.
The first drops strike and shake the stalks.
Desire attained is not desire.

The slate grey cloud comes up too fast.
However slyly we conspire,
The first drops strike and shake the stalks.
We cannot hold the thing entire.

The wind betrays its empty harvest.
The dead leaves spin and scratch the street,
Their longing for the forest
Forever incomplete.

Tell the driver to let you off
Around the corner. Be discreet.
Desire attained is not desire
But as the ashes of a fire.
The dead leaves spin and scratch the street.

The Present

For the present there is just one moon,
though every level pond gives back another.

But the bright disc shining in the black lagoon,
perceived by astrophysicist and lover,

is milliseconds old. And even that light's
seven minutes older than its source.

And the stars we think we see on moonless nights
are long extinguished. And, of course,

this very moment, as you read this line,
is literally gone before you know it.

Forget the here-and-now. We have no time
but this device of wantonness and wit.

Make me this present then: your hand in mine,
and we'll live out our lives in it.

Touch

We know she was clever because of her hands.
Hers, the first opposable thumb. Shards of her hip and skull
Suggest she was young, thirteen perhaps,
When the flash flood drowned her. Erect she stood
Lithe as a gymnast, four feet tall,

Our innocent progenitor.
Sleek-furred technician of flint and straw.
Here are her knuckle bones.

I know her touch. Though she could easily snap
My wrist, she is gentle in my dream.
She probes my face, scans my arm,
She touches my hand to know me.
Her eyes are grey in the dream, and bright.

Little mother, forgive me.
I wake you for answers in the night
Like any infant. Tell me about touch.
What necessities designed your hands and mine?
Did you kill, carve, gesture to god or gods?
Did the caress shape your hand or your hand the caress?

Music and Sex and Drinking

As a tripod stands more stable than a lectern
And lies threesquare to reason keeping level,
So three poles constitute us like dimensions:
The pebble is sexier than the owl, that drunkard,
And is all music after the final note.
All is mapped by music and sex and drinking.
Everything and each least part of everything
Each pole pulls to its own erasure
But is checked by the others,
So words keep their courtesies,
Stars keep their courses, nuclei cohere,
Till recklessly dislodged.

I find myself sobbing, over and over,
'I am exactly trivial and hold that everything,
And each least part of everything,
However tragic, chaste, tuneless, sober,
Can be accurately graphed upon these axes
To fill up its place in the world to the edges.'

'Smith'

What is this fear before the unctuous teller?
Why does it seem to take a forger's nerve
To make my signature come naturally?
Naturally? But every signature's
A trick we learn to do, consistently,
Like Queequeg's cross, or Whistler's butterfly.
Perhaps some childhood spectre grips my hand
Every time I'm asked to sign my name.

Maybe it's Sister Bridget Agatha
Who drilled her class in Christ and penmanship
And sneered *affected* at my seven-year-old scrawl.
True, it was unreadably ornate
And only one of five that I'd developed,
But try as I might I couldn't recall
The signature that I'd been born with.

Later, in my teens, I brought a girl,
My first, to see the Rodin exhibition.
I must have ranted on before each bronze;
Metal of blood and honey . . . Pure Sir Kenneth Clark.
And those were indeed the feelings I wanted to have,
But I could tell that she was unimpressed.
She fetched our coats. I signed the visitor's book,
My name embarrassed back into mere words.

No, I'm sure it all began years later.
I was twenty, and the girl was even younger.
We chose the hottest August night on record
And a hotel with no air-conditioning.
We tried to look adult. She wore her heels
And leant against the cigarette machine as,
Arching an eyebrow, I added to the register
The name I'd practised into spontaneity –
Surely it wasn't – *Mr and Mrs Smith*?

It's all so long ago and lost to me,
And yet, how odd, I remember a moment so pure,
In every infinite detail indelible,
When I gripped her small shoulders in my hands,
Steadying her in her slippery ride,
And I looked up into her half-closed eyes . . .
Dear friend, whatever is most true in me
Lives now and for ever in that instant,
The night I forged a hand, not mine, not anyone's,
And in that tiny furnace of a room,
Forged a thing unalterable as iron.

Cadenza

I've played it so often it's hardly me who plays.
We heard it that morning in Alexandria,
Or tried to, on that awful radio.
I was standing at the balustrade,
Watching the fish stalls opening on the quay,
The horizon already rippling in the heat.
She'd caught a snatch of Mozart, and was fishing
Through the static for the BBC
But getting bouzoukis, intimate Arabic,
All drowned beneath that soft roar, like the ocean's.
'Give it up,' I said, 'the tuner's broken.'
And then she crossed the room and kissed me. Later,
Lying in the curtained light, she whispered
She'd something to tell me. When all at once,
The tidal hiss we'd long since ceased to notice
Stopped. A flautist inhaled. And there it was,
The end of K285*a*,
Dubbed like a budget soundtrack on our big scene.
Next day I got the music out and learned it.

I heard it again in London a few months later,
The night she called me from the hospital.
'I've lost it,' she said, 'it happens . . .' and as she spoke
Those days in Egypt and other days returned,
Unsummoned, a tide of musics, cities, voices,
In which I drifted, helpless, disconsolate.
What did I mourn? It had no name, no sex,
'It might not even have been yours,' she said,
Or do I just imagine that she said that?

The next thing I recall, I'm in the dark
Outside St Michael's Church on Highgate Hill.
Coloured lights are strung across the portico,
Christmas lights. It's snowing on me,
And this very same cadenza – or near enough –
Rasps through a tubercular PA.
How did I get here?

Consider that radio, drifting through frequencies,
Suddenly articulate with Mozart.
Consider the soloist playing that cadenza,
Borne to the coda by his own hands.

Letter

It's stopped this morning, nine hours deep
And blank in the sun glare.
Soon the loud ploughs will drive through the drifts,
Spraying it fine as white smoke,
And give the roads back. Then I'll sleep
Knowing I've seen the blizzard through.

First your papers must be put in order.
In drawer after drawer your signatures wait
To wound me. I'll let them. There's nothing else in your hand.
No diaries, no labelled photographs, no lists.
But here's a letter you sent one year
With my name scratched carefully on onionskin.
Empty. Man of few words, you phoned to explain.
The only letter you ever wrote me
And you posted the envelope.

No relics here of how you felt;
Maybe writing frightened you, the way it fixed a whim.
Maybe ink and graphite made
Too rough a map of your fine love.
But remember one August night
When I was weak with fever and you held my head
And reeled off 'The Charge Of The Light Brigade'
(Of all things) to calm me. You had it by heart;
By breath. I'd hear that breath when you talked to yourself
Spitting tiny curses, or muttered in your sleep,
Or read, as monks and rabbis do, aloud, soft.
Breath that would hardly steam a mirror,
Whispering like gaslight. Day after year
After night I missed the words.

I always will. Of the funeral I recall
Only overcoats, a grey priest droning
'*The letter kills*', *said Paul*,
'*The spirit giveth life.*' And my breath,
Held, jaw clamped, the long drive home . . .

Three weeks have passed. Three weeks the clouds clenched
Low in the sky, too cold to snow until last night
When I rose to the slap of sleet on the glass and hard wind
And saw my face lamplit in the dark window,
Startled that I looked older, more like you.
Then half asleep, half frozen, close up against the pane, I mouthed
Father. Frost fronds quickly swirled and vanished
As if you read them back to me. Your breath
Making the blizzard silent,
The silence quiet, at last,
The quiet ours.

Shibboleth

One didn't know the name of Tarzan's monkey.
Another couldn't strip the cellophane
From a GI's pack of cigarettes.
By such minutiae were the infiltrators detected.

By the second week of battle
We'd become obsessed with trivia.
At a sentry point, at midnight, in the rain,
An ignorance of baseball could be lethal.

The morning of the first snowfall, I was shaving,
Staring into a mirror nailed to a tree,
Intoning the Christian names of the Andrews Sisters.
'Maxine, Laverne, Patty.'

Quorum

In today's *Guardian*, the word *quorum*
is spelled the same as *oqürum*,
the only surviving word of Khazar,
according to the *Great Soviet Encyclopaedia*.
Oqürum, meaning 'I have read'.

The original pronunciation is lost for ever,
but I weigh three syllables in my palm
against 'paprika' and 'samovar',
'cedarwood' and, for some reason,
'mistletoe'. I have read . . .

an entire literature,
and enacted all that it describes.
On a winter morning, in an ochre room
that we can never enter, the resonance
of those imaginary consonants

the elders whisper over ancient documents
flickers the blood bright shadow
from a glass of tea.

Auto da Fé

Last night I met my uncle in the rain
And he told me he'd been dead for fifty years.
My parents told me he'd been shot in Spain
Serving with the Irish volunteers.
But in this dream we huddled round a brazier
And passed the night in heated argument.
'El sueño de razón . . . ' and on it went.
And as he spoke he rolled a cigarette
And picked a straw and held it to an ember.
The shape his hand made sheltering the flame
Was itself a kind of understanding.
But it would never help me to explain
Why my uncle went to fight for Spain,
For Christ, for the Caudillo, for the King.

Ramon Fernandez?

I met him when I fought in the brigade,
In Barcelona, when the people had it.

Red flags snapped above the tower clock
Of what had been renamed the 'Lenin Barracks'.
The ancient face was permanently fixed,
If memory serves, at half eleven.
Dead right twice a day.

Fernandez played guitar each day at noon
In the plaza beneath the barracks tower,
Hawking his revolutionary broadsides.
And as he sang he stared up at the clock
As if he half expected it to move.

I recall the way he played the crowd
Sure as he played his lacquered blue guitar.
I recall the troop trains pulling from the station,
White knuckles over carbines, boys' voices
Singing the anthems of Ramon Fernandez.

And I wonder if anyone caught on but me.
The songs the fascists sang across the wire
Were his, the same he sang, got us to sing.
A few words changed, not many. *Libertad*,
Hermana Libre, I have them all by heart.

One day he vanished back across the front
And later, when the town was under siege,
A stray round hit the barracks clock and cracked
Both iron hands clean off but left the face
To glare like a phase of the moon above the burning city.

Partisans

Imagine them labouring selflessly,
Gathering evidence through the long winter.
Now they bring their case before you.
'Let us arrive at the truth together'

They say, these patient women and men.
The seconds tick by in the small cell.
The fluorescent bulb whines like a dentist's drill.
They want you to spell the names again.

Majority

Foreign policy does not exist for us.
We don't know where the new countries are.
We don't care. We want the streets safe
So we vote for the chair. An eye for an eye.

Our long boats will come in the spring
And we will take many heads.
The name of our tribe means 'human being'.
We will make your children pray to our god in public.

News item

The trampled corpses
Stacked in the lobby
Are all that remain of the literal-minded.

Among the missing
Are the little girl who shouted 'Fire'
And those of us who remained seated
Savouring the sheer
Theatre.

Pornography

The bodies of giants shine before us like a crowded fire.
One might quite credibly shout 'Theatre'.
I can't watch this. Instead, I'll stare at the projector beam
The smoke and dust revolve in and reveal.

Remember my story?
How one grey dawn in Maine I watched from my car
As a goshawk dove straight down toward the pines?
I said the dive was there before the hawk was,
Real as a wind shear before the blown snow reveals it.
The hawk became its aim, made one smooth purchase
In a splintering of twigs. A hare squealed, and I watched the bird
Slam the air in vain till it gave up and dropped its catch.
I told you how I sat and watched the rabbit die,
And described blood steaming on the frosted gravel.

Remember how angry you were
When I told you I'd made it up?
That I'd never been to Maine or owned a car?
But I told my tale well, bought your pity for the hare,
Terror for the hawk, and I served my point,
Whatever it was.

And remember that time
I was trapped in a cave and saw shadows on the limestone wall?
When the scouts freed me and carried me to the cave mouth
The true light burned my eyes like acid. Hours passed
Before I found myself safe in the Maine woods, resting in my car.

THE END is near. The final frame of *Triumph of the Will*
Slips past the lens and the blank flash blinds us.

Footage from the Interior

I

Boyoko is teaching me to wait.
We squat behind wrist-thick
Stalks of palm and listen
For the faint drumming of engines.

Just after sundown
The trawler slides around the headland.
The motor coughs, whinnies, and stops.
We watch and wait

As one by one the running lights
Go out across the dark lagoon.
Voices carry from the deck across the still water.
Not the words, but the sweep and glide of words.

Theirs is a tongue of tones and cadences
And Boyoko knows from the rhythm alone
Whether to slip away unseen
Or wait for rifles.

II

Boyoko is teaching me Lekele.
'Our word for *lagoon*
Can also mean *poison*, or *promise*,
Depending on the syllable stressed.'

A blue moth thrums
The windscreen of the idling jeep,
Slamming its tiny head against the glass
In urgent Morse.

Boyoko beats the word *freedom*
On the steering wheel.
'Try it.' I try it.
'No,' he tells me, 'you said *bacon*.'

III

Boyoko's been teaching me the 'talking drums'.
Side by side, we stand among the chickens
In the yard behind his hut.
I'm roasting. And my fingers ache.

Today when his son walked past
Boyoko lost me, slapping rhythm
Over rhythm. I stopped, he smiled,
And we resumed our lesson.

Minutes passed,
And then the boy came back
Bringing two cans of cold brown beer.

Khalypso

The development of complex cell communities in the zygote thus resembles the creation of heavier and heavier elements in the star's contraction . . .

– R. Profitendieu, *Birth*

Cast off old love like substance from a flame;
Cast off that ballast from your memory.
But leave me and you leave behind your name.

When snows have made ideas of the rain,
When canvas bloats and ships grow on the sea,
Cast off old love like substance from a flame.

Your eyes are green with oceans and you strain
To crown and claim your sovereignty,
You leave me and you leave behind your name

And all the mysteries these isles retain.
But if the god of sailors hacks you free,
Cast off old love like substance from a flame

Until you're in a woman's bed again
And make her moan as you make me,
'Leave me and you leave behind your name.'

The brails go taut. The halyard jerks, the pain
Of breeching to the squall and all to be
Cast off, old love, like substance from a flame.
Now leave me. I will live behind your name.

The Bacchae

Look out, Slim, these girls are trouble.
You dance with them they dance you back.
They talk it broad but they want it subtle
and you got too much mouth for that.
Their secret groove's their sacred grove –
not clever not ever, nor loud, nor flaunt.
I know you, Slim, you're a jerk for love.
The way you talk is the what you want.
You want numbers. You want names.
You want to cheat at rouge et noir.
But these are initiated dames –
the how they move is the what they are.

A Disaster

We were ships in the night.
We thought her rockets were fireworks.

Our radio was out, and we didn't know
The band was only playing to calm the passengers.

Christ, she was lovely all lit up,
Like a little diamond necklace!

Try to understand. Out here in the dark
We thought we were missing the time of our lives.

We could almost smell her perfume.
And she went down in sight of us.

Starlet

Berenice affects her April dialect.
Buds bloom stiffly to her rapid vowels, mud breaks
For apple-green shoots. Nude, descending
A staircase, she trails a shady wake of geometries
Like a ship stirring shoals of luminous algae.
Freely she warms to the folk whose soles
Thump brownly on her marble floors.
She breathes their garlic air wheezed
From hot concertinas and, in the cool evening,
She unbinds her starry skein of hair,
The heavens bespangling with dishevelled light,
Gives interviews.

Interviews

Yvette lets a drop
Of red blot brilliant
On the white,
Fresh bedsheet.

1913. She looks up
From painting her toenails.
Marcel is ahead of his time,
Yvette is still dressing.

He finds a note
From Apollinaire:
'Knight to
Queen's rook three.'

And checks the board.
He looks at the little horse, snaps
It across the room,
A distance

> *Of fifty years*
> *To a studio in Neuilly*
> *Cassette wheels spinning*
> *Throughout the interview*
> *And he thinks of bicycles.*

Q: *Where does your anti-retinal attitude come from?*
A: *From too great an importance given to the retina.*

1913. It's getting late.
The sun obscures
As it illuminates
Garden and gardener
Whose hedge-clippers snip . . .

'Zip me,'
Yvette says over her shoulder,
Stepping into her yellow pumps,

The ones with the goldfish in the heels.

> *Wait, I'll flip*
> *The cassette to erase*
> *'Interview with Delta bluesman*
> *Son House 1/5/68'*

Q: *What about Willie, was he very good at making up verses?*
A: *Yeh, he could make up verses pretty good. Yeh, 'cause he'd start on one thing he'd let near about every word be pertaining to what he pronounced what he was going to play about. That's the difference in him and Charley and me, too. Charley, he could start singing of the shoe there and wind up singing about that banana.*

Marcel looks at the little horse
And wonders whether
'Nude Descending a Staircase'
Is the name of his entry
In the armoury show

Or if 'Nude Descending a Staircase'
Is his entry
In the armoury show.

Within three years
His friends will drop in the trench
Screaming, chlorine searing
Their throats and noses raw.
Apollinaire in the field-hospital,
Red on white gauze,
Will imagine the random trajectories
Of fragments, shrapnel, chessmen.

A: *Since Courbet, it's been believed that painting is addressed to the retina. Before, painting had other functions: it could be . . . moral.*

> Stop.

I'd be playin' by myself sometime, nobody will be around me whatever
to hear it, and my mind will be settin' on some crazy things – Scripture
or jes names of songs, any old thing. 'Fore I know anything tears'll be
coming down and I put that guitar away.

Back from the Salon,
Yvette removes
Her yellow shoes.
The gramophone
Clears its throat
For Satie.

Yvette, Yvette,
So much to drink.

From tonight on you'll be Rrose,
Rrose Selavy.

Later he'll undress her.
Setting long glove

And stocking down at right
Angles. Here comes

The bride.

> *Duchamp then produced*
> *A miniature machine for me*
> *To photograph: watch parts*
> *Clicking and skidding*
> *Across clear, flat glass*
> *Toward two gnat-sized yellow shoes.*

But now they laugh in the dark.
Lighting her cigarette,

Marcel makes a world around them,
A short, shining world.

Remembering Steps to Dances Learned Last Night

Massive my heart, the heart of a hero, I knew it,
Though I was ten, pimpled, squint eyed, dung spattered.
I strung a bow, and memorized a brief heroic song
(I'll sing it for you later), left my goats in my father's yard,
And then went down to the ship.
Many men massed at the dock, loud their laughter.
But the king listened, noted my name, gave me wine,
A little patriotic speech, and sent me home
To the goats and the tedium and the ruminant years.
Once I made a song about the king and his distant plundering
And the hoard of memories, wondrous, he was gathering.
It's a shame you didn't bring your guitar.

Then one summer, when I was older,
And the king was long since missing in action,
Men came from Achaia to court the lonely queen.
The nights got loud with drums and laughter echoing from the
    palace,
Women's laughter, and the smell of roasted lamb.
What would you have done? I pounded on the gates one morning,
Rattled my arrows and stamped and sang about my hero-heart.
They seemed to understand . . . Or didn't mind my lying,
And they opened the gates on another world.
Beauty. Deception. Of weaving, of magic, and of the edge of the
    known world
When the light fails, and you fall dead drunk across the table,
All these we learned in our feasts and games amid the grey-eyed
    women.
Clever men and many we waited, the queen to choose among.

I know you came to hear me sing about the night the king came
    home,
When hero slaughtered hero in the rushlit hall,
Blood speckling the white clay walls wine dark.
I can't. I'd stepped outside when the music stopped mid-tune.
Alone in the dark grove, I heard no sound but distant insects,
And the sound of water, mine, against the palace wall.
And then I heard their screams, the men and women I'd spent that
    summer with.

What would you have done?
I staggered home in the dawn rain, still half drunk,
Forgetting one by one the names of my dead friends,
Remembering steps to dances learned that night,
that very night,
Back to my goats, goat stink, goat cheese, the governing of goats.

The Tuning

If anyone asks you how I died, say this:
The angel of death came in the form of a moth
And landed on the lute I was repairing.
I closed up shop
And left the village on the quietest night of summer,
The summer of my thirtieth year,
And went with her up through the thorn forest.

Tell them I heard yarrow stalks snapping beneath my feet
And heard a dog bark far off, far off.
That's all I saw or heard,
Apart from the angel at ankle level leading me,
Until we got above the beeline and I turned
To look for the last time on the lights of home.

That's when she started singing.
It's written that the voice of the god of Israel
Was the voice of many waters.
But this was the sound of trees growing,
The noise of a pond thrown into a stone.

When I turned from the lights below to watch her sing,
I found the angel changed from moth to woman,
Singing inhuman intervals through her human throat,
The notes at impossible angles justified.

If you understand, friend, explain to them
So they pray for me. How could I go back?
How could I bear to hear the heart's old triads –
Clatter of hooves, the closed gate clanging,
A match scratched toward a pipe –
How could I bear to hear my children cry?

I found a rock that had the kind of heft
We weigh the world against
And brought it down fast against my forehead
Again, again, until blood drenched my chest
And I was safe and real forever.

Rational Construction

Along a girder, high above the pavement
A man is carrying a man-length mirror.
Crowds gather to track his movements,
His one foot easing over the other.
We squint, and the sun snaps down from the glass
Finding faces. But up there they keep
Their eyes on their feet. We bask in their flash,
But they owe us no 'intuitive leap'.

The Dreamer and the Dreamed Have Dinner

Rien n'est, en effet, plus désenchantant, plus pénible, que de
regarder, après des années, ses phrases. Elles se sont en quelque
sorte décantées et déposent au fond du livre; et, la plupart du
temps les volumes ne sont pas ainsi que les vins qui s'améliorent
en vieillissant; une fois dépouillés par l'âge, les chapitres s'éven-
tent, et leur bouquet s'étiole.

– Huysmans

It is the ripest hour. He stands before the window,
Scans the night and sighs, clouding the pane.
Road. Streetlamps. Shops. The solstice light
Smooths a pool of similes disguised as names.
His carafe, half drained, opaque in the dark,
Conceals before it is uncorked and poured.
Beyond mere sense, so does his heart
Until the clock, clicks locked in random clusters,
Resolves arhythmically. Chuck: a car door?
'Her Citroën,' he thinks, because he trusts her
Cycles and her secret female arts.
All wines retain impurities. A sip
Numbs an unexamined intention as she knocks.
His welcomes are readied with overkill workmanship.

'Late again.' They talk. They spend the twilight
On his terrace rereading *Against the Grain*.
'Like tears in different colours . . .' (She *abhors*
It when he does this. Large drops of warm rain
Dapple their shoulders, so they drift indoors.)
She stretches and yawns; he persists unaware . . .
'Like gazing at a photographic detail
Of a wineglass, unable to say what it is.'
Why must he slow the sunset with these flares?

'Oh for a beaker full of the warm south,'
She offers. Stumped, he laughs for sheer decorum.
Nothing slowly happens. Their shadows stretch out
In a half-light charged with visionary boredom:
Pale whims, faint furies, dim endeavours
Await the age's end, the commonsense of darkness.
When will darkness come? When will the lovers?

Seven Poems from the Welsh

Sion ap Brydydd (d. 1360) was a contemporary of the undisputed master of classical Welsh poetry, Dafydd ap Gwilym, and it is in the shadow of Dafydd's achievement that Sion's significance has been so unfortunately obscured. A commoner by birth, Sion borrowed a sum from the court of Owain for his education to the career of court poet. He held that post for less than a year when he was dismissed for neglecting to repay the loan and he spent his remaining years among the criminal element of Aberystwyth. Perhaps as a result, his diction is a mixture of poetic 'mandarin' Welsh and earthy demotic. And this, together with his obsessive use of difficult forms, has marked him as an eccentric in the history of Welsh poetry. For example, recent computer analysis of *Y Hiraeth*, his 30,000-word description of the interior of a heron's egg, has revealed two columns of slant rhyme weaving through the text line by line in a perfect double helix pattern. How such a poem could have been written under such exacting formal constraints is a puzzle. Why it was written is a positive enigma.

He is best known, however, for his 30-syllable *englynion*. These short poems were not *composed* in the sense in which that term applies to the writing of English poetry. Rather, they were thought to have *obtained*, like Japanese *tanka* and *haiku*, as the complete and inevitable response to a split second of painfully acute perception. To the objection that the preconceived form of the poem shapes that perception, Sion would answer that during such moments neither poet, poem, nor subject can be distinguished one from the other. In this mysterious way, he believed, all his englynion were faint echoes of a single unwritten poem which, if pronounced, would so perfectly unite the souls of author and listener that they would inhabit each other's bodies and exchange destinies. This poem, he believed, drifted just beyond his grasp 'like a snowflake of complex geometry which dissolves when it lights on the tongue'.

In the winter of 1360 Sion was beheaded for the crime of adultery. Here are my translations of seven in a sequence of twenty-nine englynion he wrote in the tower of Pentraeth on the eve of his execution.

I

Morfydd, daughter of Gwyn,
The dells are bright with snow.
Driven with cruel purity,
They'll take you for one of their own.

II

Cloves and cedar smoke in the air,
Swarms of dragonflies in the long grass.
I unlaced her muslin gown.
No help from her.

III

Smooth the skin on a bowl of milk
And on the warm hollow of her thigh.
The soft turf is slow to warm,
And after this, shallow breathing.

IV

The moment you touch the whorl of my ear
With the tip of your tongue
Is a gold dome over itself.
So is the moment after.

XXVII

Dull the journey.
Feeble and muttering the old men.
Amber and sweet the wine of spring.
I won't have autumn's vinegar.

XXVIII

Dull the journey.
Long the road reeled in toward the lantern.
Patience is cold soup
And salt in the sugar bowl.

XXIX

Say this rhyme, reader, aloud to yourself.
Gladly I'd bear your senility and incontinence,
Let you warm this bed of hay,
Rattle these chains, write these lines.

The Toast

You may have glimpsed a version of the Toast – our most curious tradition – played by our children on the streets of your cities at twilight, or seen, at our weddings, the young men dressed in red shot silk, wineglasses balanced brim-full on the backs of their hands, shuffling the intricate steps whilst reciting the tongue-twisting parable of the tailor's thimble.

The age and meaning of the Toast are much disputed. Heraklius contends that the ritual is merely a corruption of a trick schoolboys once used to remember the names and dates of our country's defeats. It will be noted that Heraklius is a northerner. A more promising avenue of investigation lies in the fact that, 'the thimble', familiar to us from the nursery as part of the dandling-song of the infant prince exposed on the hillside and raised by fieldmice, is in fact a rebus for remembering the constellations, and the accurate dancing of the toast was a skill much prized among our seafaring ancestors who chanted the story to navigate, stomping the deckboards and raising ladles of fresh water to the Pole Star.

And it was said to be once a trial for witches or spies from the north who, unable to mimic the nimble steps and rhymes would trip up, drop the chalice, and seal their fates. And some scholars say that the story is only a code for the steps of another dance, long since forgotten, but often depicted in the *goblet-bearing youth* motif of our pottery.

The Natural and Social Sciences

We come to Straidkilly to watch the tide go out.
A man is loading a wicker basket
With small, complicated pink crabs.
'Have we missed it,' we ask, 'the tide?'
And he, with sincere assurance,
'It'll be back.'

A girl inspects an upside-down bike
On the road to Tubbercurry.
I stop to help but she rights it on its wheels,
Shoves off, ticking in the light rain.

Musicians in the kitchen, Sunday morning in Gweedore.
An American with a tape recorder and a yellow notebook.
'What was the name of that last one?'
The piper shrugs and points to the dark corner.
'Ask my father.'
The American writes 'Ask My Father'.

The Last Tea of Rikyu

Early evening and a summer presence.
A moist wind moves on the roofs of Horyu-Ji,
Flicks iridescent beetle wings beneath wrought copper;
It is the daily rainstorm.

But we are in the tea hut in Rikyu's garden.
Rikyu, slandered without grace or respect,
Condemned by a dull and intolerant patron,
Is granted an hour of life.

The whirr of insects,
The master's hands, the lanterns,
And the damp hiss of the kettle
Show forth from the moment.

We take our places.
    'Do not be sad.
    We will meet every time there is tea.'
The unsteady cup warms my hands.

The others withdraw like shadows.
I remain to witness the gesture.
Rikyu unwraps bands of black silk
From the short sword.

His eyes are clear.
    'Have we not already died
    Who live beyond fear and desire?'
I weep for humility and gratitude

And do not see the shock, the body buckling.
This is how it always begins;
A jolt, the world whirls within us,
A raindrop hesitates, then hits the roof.

The Noh

After 1868 when the Shogunate was overthrown and the Noh
fell out of favour, the costumers and mask makers who had pre-
viously produced so many rich effects became careless in their
productions, offering only a few crude variations.

– Yamashiro, *A History of Noh*

From the bright glass greenhouse steamed with palms
She brings you from sleep to where she has tacked
A mask of wood to a trellis arm
To seduce you. She *is* abstract.

Thunderstorms tonight, she warns.
No stars suspend above the palms
But gro-lights crackle on the leathery leaves.
Tonight, in her arms,

Conquer the noble opacity of the mask
Back to its maker who planed the cheapest wood
Against the grain and pilfered the design
Arse deep in debt and carving against a deadline.

His early masks were perfect. So were mine.
But roles come and go, standards and wood decay
And split. One can no longer say,
'Had we but world enough and time',

You just make do. Unclench your fists.
This delicate cheek and skin of painted pine
Provide your mind for silence by themselves.
He taught no truth to shape who chiselled this.

The gong tolls classically. It is twelve,
And the drops against the glass become a hiss.
Kiss her. Her rhythmic breathing levels
Beyond her name and beauty to a 'yes'.
Together leave the greenhouse its emptiness.

Inheritance

My father would have cherished an heir,
but he remained unmarried.

Science was his mistress, and after science,
my mother. But we were provided

with a collection of seashells
second only to the emperor's.

I regret I will not live
to see the final specimen auctioned.

It is the jewel in the diadem.
A sulphur nautilus,

wound like the spring of a gold watch.
My mother would not part with it in life.

When he died I saw his name
in the *Journal of Marine Genetics*. Sharp,

peach-coloured spikes of coral
are named for him.

The Origin of Geometry

High above Thebes the huge birds glide
Describing smaller and smaller circles.
Below, the Greek boy tells his teacher

That all things, the cinnamon air at dusk
And the red sand, are the 3D
Writing of the gods.

Just so, he says, his alphabet's a world
Dug in red sand with a cypress stick.
He stands above it like a god.

But the old man carves pictures
On a lump of clay. Moon. Scarab.
'See? See?' Young Thales points

To the first letter of his name.
'Round like the moon.' The old man squints
Brushing a fly from his face.

In just a moment
They will lose the gods for ever.
But now the cranes fly round and round

Into the maelstrom of the lengthening light.

The Penitent

At times also I have been put to confusion and driven to despair
of ever explaining something for which I could not account, but
which my senses told me to be true.

– Galileo Galilei, *Two New Sciences*

Unseen, dogs cough on the colourless beach
Over waves, incessant, incessant. If all this sand
Were dried and ground and polished to a lens
That order now fanned out too far
For us to see could focus through it.
But see, they subside, Procyon and the Twins.
Defaced by day, their imagined musculature
Crushes and sharpens a tiny brilliance on my sin,
Igniting kindling. My eyes are stung with smoke;
Too much truth in too grey a place
And too combustible a heart. These days
I move in quiet circles and take for nourishment
Light's white gristle, the unprismed lie.
God shines. The tide looks solid in his love,
And yet it *does* move.

The Don't Fall Inn

The blue pool illuminated, the cocktail lounge is open.
Rippling with liquid glints like firelight,
The lit bellhop gazes in terror
At the diving board and the cool, deep mirror.

Here is the Register of Revelations.
Use my pen. 'Edvard . . . and . . . Mimi . . . Munch.'
We hear muffled voices through the walls.
A strangely submarine effect. Like bubbles.

Something is terribly wrong
And the porters come to dust it.
They are hoovering as we leave at dawn.
Although the word 'TV' is out,
They flash the sign against the hail grey sky:
REASONABLE RATES   OLYMPIC SIZE POOL
                  . . . IN EVERY ROOM
Goodbye.

Riddle

I am the book you'll never read
But carry
For ever,

One blunt page, garlanded
By daughter
Or lover.

You already know two-thirds by heart.
And I'm passing weighty for a work so short.

Envoi

Go away. All that's over.
No more fluttering, squirming, crawling, running.
I've achieved stillness, clarity.
Since the tide gave up this one rock
And I'm the only point to reckon by
Many of you have taken me for a sign.
Stop. Stay on the deep.
Wing back down the round sleep of waters.
Deceive them, tell them it never ends.
Give me peace.

But the speech of skulls is strange to birds.
Weary, eager for crumbs and Noah's praise,
The dove snapped half the glittering twig
Curling green in the eye socket,
Clutched it, flew.

ERRATA

Contents

I. *Places in the Temple*

Held

Not in the sense that this snapshot, a girl in a garden,
Is named for its subject, or saves her from ageing,
Not as this ammonite changed like a sinner to minerals
Heavy and cold on my palm is immortal,
But as we stopped for the sound of the lakefront one morning
Before the dawn chorus of sprinklers and starlings.

Not as this hieroglyph chiselled by Hittites in lazuli,
Spiral and faint, is a word for 'unending',
Nor as the hands, crown, and heart in the emblem of Claddagh,
Pewter and plain on that ring mean forever,
But as we stood at the window together, in silence,
Precisely twelve minutes by candlelight waiting for thunder.

Acts of Contrition

There's you, behind the red curtain,
waiting to absolve me in the dark.
Here's me, third in the queue outside
the same deep green velvet curtain.
I'm working on my confessional tone.

Here's me opening my wrists
before breakfast, Christmas day,
and here's you asking if it hurt.
Here's where I choose between *mea culpa*
and *Why the hell should I tell you?*

Me again, in the incident room this time,
spitting my bloody teeth into your palm.
I could be anyone you want me to be.
I might come round to your point of view.

The Incense Contest

Are you awake, my sweet barbarian?
Why, you look as though you'd seen a ghost!
Are you so shocked to see a lady smoke?
I owe this habit to the Prince, my husband.
That interests you? But that was years ago,
When high-born women told the time by crickets
And generals burned perfumes in their helmets
The night before they rode their troops to battle.
Among the rich it was considered proper
For gentlemen to keep some trace of court
About them in the sweat and shit and smoke.
Among our set those days, in fact, the game
Of 'Guess the Incense' was the latest rage.
Played, like all our games, in grace and earnest,
By intricate directions, for high stakes.

And crispest winter evenings were the best
Because the air is cleanest in the cold.
Without music, badinage, or flowers,
With all attention focused on the flame,
We'd kneel and sniff, and sigh in recognition,
Or we'd pretend, to save a reputation,
Or gamble on assent when someone twigged
'Why this is *Plum Tree Blossom* mixed with balsam.'
On such a night the Empress proposed
An incense contest for the Heian ladies.

We worked for weeks refining subtleties
Of clove and cinnamon and sandalwood,
Selecting lacquers for the bowls and burners
And stiff kimonos for our serving girls.
Imagine generals in midnight camps
Nudging sticks and pebbles across maps;
Just so we worried over strategies
Until the evening of the second snow.

That night we drank the Empress's *sake*.
The Prince, my husband, danced and spoke
A poem written by my grandfather:

> *Shadows on your screens;*
> *a document inked in script*
> *I will yet master.*

A very famous poem. You smile, my lord,
But I come from a literary line.

The alcove, I recall, was full of courtiers
Brushing snow from silken hunting vests
And ladies hushing them. A fan was flicked
To signify the contest had commenced.

First my cousin knelt above the brazier
And blent two scents together on the fire.
Eagles in Winter Light, I think,
And *Village of the Pines* with bergamot.
At first I found her effort elegant,
Warm and old and calm. But moments later,
Barbed and pungent with an old resentment.
The Empress nodded, and glancing toward my husband
Misquoted one of my grandfather's lines.

Next my sister burnt an amber resin
Suggesting pavements after summer rain.
We all felt something which we couldn't name
But which we all agreed was sad and cold
And distant, like some half-remembered grief
From girlhood, or a herb like marjoram.
Once more her Majesty addressed the Prince,
'You seem to have remarkably broad taste.'
And looked at me with something worse than pity.
I knew I'd lost. And when it was my turn
To add my clichéd fragrance to the fire
A door slid open deep within my head . . .

But how can I describe what happened then?
Except to say the blind must dream. They smell
And touch and taste and hear; and you, my dear,
Can dream – are dreaming even now, perhaps –
While all about you swirls a hidden world
Where memories contend like hungry ghosts.
I didn't smell my incense in the brazier:
I smelled the forest and I smelled the horses,
The dung in stables, women giving birth,
The rotting teeth of footmen from the provinces,
The coppery reek of blood, the clogged latrines,
The foetid corpses of the foreign priests
My husband crucified at Gyotoku.
I smelled so many women on the Prince
I smelled the Prince on every woman there.

Are you awake? For if it please you, lord,
To hold that candle just beneath my pipe
Until the black tar glows . . .
                                    There. I smoke
To keep those smells at bay. It isn't free,
My dear barbarian, so don't forget
To demonstrate that generosity
For which your noble race is celebrated.
The crickets signal dawn. Time to rise
And face the sun and leave me to my dream.

Glass

This is a cheapjack gift at the year's end.
This is a double-glazing hymn for wind.
This is a palm frond held out to a friend
Who holds her lifeline lightly in her hand.

As fine sand filaments the unclenched hand
Or leaves the palm grit-filmed but crazed, lines end
Across prismatic windscreens. Every friend
A meteorologist's diagram of wind.

Blow smoke into the fist of either hand
And pull it tight and loop it round the end
Of every night held up by wine and friend,
Sootflecked and leaning on a London wind,

Then say our ribboned smoke's erased by wind,
Our glass is sand. You start, but in the end,
Somehow, I stay. You stay, somehow, my friend
Who grips me tightest in her open hand.

The Commission

In spring when the mountain snows melt
and the western wind crumbles
and loosens the clods, in the spring
when the bees roam incontinently
over the glades and the woodlands,
I returned to the plague-levelled city
to cut off the head of the man
who had murdered my brother.

To cover my purpose and pay off my debts
I set up a shop in the Via Rigoglio
and accepted a papal commission.
In the evenings I shadowed
the arquebusier Ludovico
like a love-smitten boy,
watching his house,
his comings and goings.

Pope Clement had ordered three follies:
a spindly gold locust that chirruped and kicked
on release of a mainspring,
an amethyst brooch,
and a nine-inch stiletto
with monogrammed handle in findrinny
and he wanted a cameo laid in its pommel:
Hercules binding the three-headed Cerberus.

To help me I hired a silversmith
known as Filippo, whose idiot daughter
I kept in the shop to amuse me. But
during that summer she fell in a fever.
Her hand was diseased. Both the bones of her thumb
and ring finger were eaten away.
I'd received an advance from the Pope
so I sent for the finest of surgeons.

She screamed when he started
to scrape away some of the bone
using a crude iron tool, and since
I could see he was making no progress
I got him to stop for five minutes. I ran
to the workshop and fashioned
a delicate instrument, steel, curved,
tiny and sharp as a razor.

This I gave to the surgeon
who now worked so gently
the girl felt no pain.
Filippo in gratitude made me a gift
of a dagger he'd chanced on in Persia.
He knew I would find the design on the handle
compelling – the name of their god
swirling like silvery foliage.

(The ignorant call such engravings 'grotesques'
because they resemble the carvings in grottoes.
This is an error. For just as the ancients
created their monsters
by mating with bulls and with horses,
so we artists create our own monsters
in networks of intertwined branches and leaves.)

I finally found Ludovico alone
on the night of the feast of St Mark.
It was pissing down rain and the bells
of S. Paolo were striking eleven.
I crept up behind as he stood
in a doorway in Torre Sanguigna
and brought down the silversmith's dagger
as hard as I could on his nape

but he turned and I shattered his shoulder.
Blinded with pain he let go of his sword
and again I went straight for his neck,
and this time the blade stuck so deep that it snapped
at the hilt. Then he fell to his knees
and stared at me stupidly, clutching the knife
as if he were trying to keep me away from it.
I looked in his eyes until I was sure they were empty.
Then footsteps. I broke off the handle and ran.

I was suspected of course, so I kept out of sight
and worked day and night for the Pope
as I had no desire to spend August in Rome
or get myself hanged.
When I finally brought him his toys
he was propped up in bed
being bled. But he granted an audience.
Jaundice. His flesh was like cheese.

When I laid out my labours before him
he squinted and sent for his spectacles,
then for more lamps. But it was no use.
He was blind as a mole.
Most of the time he spent sighing
and praising my God-given talent,
thumbing that wretched mechanical insect.

He almost ignored the stiletto
on which, from the figure of Hercules down,
I'd copied the Persian device from the dagger
that brought me such luck, disguising
the writing as branches.

By Christmas Pope Clement was dead.
And all of my efforts to stay in his favour
were wasted, which just goes to show
how completely the stars rule our lives.

Cruising Byzantium

The saved, say firemen, sometimes return,
Enduring the inferno of the flat
To fetch the family photos. And they burn
Not for cash, cashmere coat, nor cat,
Nor, as they momently suppose, for love.
They perish for the heraldries of light
And not such lives as these are emblem of.
But the saved, say firemen, are sometimes right.

Have you seen our holiday snaps from Greece?
Each Virgin burns in incandescent wonder
From her gold mosaic altarpiece.
This one was smashed by Gothic boot boys under
Orders from an Emperor who burned
The icon painters for idolatry.
Before her ruined face the faithful learned
The comet's path to a celestial sea.
And look. Here's *you* in skintight scuba gear
Winking through the window of your mask!
You have become the fetish that you wear.
I know precisely what you're going to ask;
Though golden in the Adriatic haze
You've waded to your thighs in molten light,
Your second skin aglitter in the sprays,
Your first it was we brought to bed that night.
And yet I'd almost brave the flames to keep
This idyll of perversity from burning.

Each photo frames a door beyond which, deep
Within the Patriarchate of my yearning,
The marble pavements surge with evensong.
But firemen say the saved are sometimes wrong.

City of God

When he failed the seminary he came back home
to the Bronx and sat in a back pew
of St Mary's every night reciting the Mass
from memory – quietly, continually –
into his deranged overcoat.
He knew the local phone book off by heart.
He had a system, he'd explain,
perfected by Dominicans in the Renaissance.

To every notion they assigned a saint,
to every saint an altar in a transept of the church.
Glancing up, column by column, altar by altar,
they could remember any prayer they chose.
He'd used it for exams, but the room went wrong –
a strip-lit box exploding slowly as he fainted.
They found his closet papered floor to ceiling
with razored passages from St Augustine.

He needed a perfect cathedral in his head,
he'd whisper, so that by careful scrutiny
the mind inside the cathedral inside the mind
could find the secret order of the world
and remember every drop on every face
in every summer thunderstorm.
And that, he'd insist, looking beyond you,
is why he came home.

I walked him back one evening as the snow
hushed the precincts of his vast invisible temple.
Here was Bruno Street where Bernadette
collapsed, bleeding through her skirt
and died, he had heard, in a state of mortal sin;

here, the site of the bakery fire where Peter stood
screaming on the red-hot fire escape,
his bare feet blistering before he jumped;
and here the storefront voodoo church beneath the el
where the Cuban *bruja* bought black candles,
its window strange with plaster saints and seashells.

Liverpool

Ever been tattooed? It takes a whim of iron,
takes sweating in the antiseptic-stinking parlour,
nothing to read but motorcycle magazines
before the blood-sopped cotton and, of course, the needle,
all for – at best – some Chinese dragon.
But mostly they do hearts,

hearts skewered, blurry, spurting like the Sacred Heart
on the arms of bikers and sailors.
Even in prison they get by with biro ink and broken glass,
carving hearts into their arms and shoulders.
But women's are more intimate. They hide theirs,
under shirts and jeans, in order to bestow them.

Like Tracy, who confessed she'd had hers done
one legless weekend with her ex.
Heart. Arrow. Even the bastard's initials, R.J.L.,
somewhere where it hurt, she said,
and when I asked her where, snapped 'Liverpool'.

Wherever it was, she'd had it sliced away
leaving a scar, she said, pink and glassy,
but small, and better than having his mark on her,

(that self-same mark of Valentinus,
who was flayed for love, but who never
 – so the cardinals now say – existed.
Desanctified, apocryphal, like Christopher,
like the scar you never showed me, Trace,
your (   ), your ex, your 'Liverpool').

Still, when I unwrap the odd anonymous note
I let myself believe that it's from you.

L

'Switch off the engine and secure the car.'
He slots his pen across his clipboard
and makes a little cathedral of his fingers
as though I were helping him with his enquiries.
'Tell me, Michael, what's your line of work?'

I tell him the truth. Why not? I've failed anyway.
'Driving and writing have a lot in common,'
he parleys, and we sit there, the two of us
blinking into the average braking distance
for 30 mph, wondering what he means.

I want to help but it's his turn to talk.
When my turn comes he'll probably look at me
instead of his hand, stalled now in mid-gesture
like a milkfloat halfway across a junction.
Look at him. What if I'd said *butcher*?

At last 'It's all a matter of giving – proper – signals'
is the best he can do. But then he astonishes me.
'I'm going to approve your licence,
but I don't care much for your . . .' Quick glance.
'*interpretation* of the Highway Code.'

Alas, Alice,

who woke to crows and woke up on the ceiling and hung there fearing the evening's sweeping and looked down now at her unfinished reading and loved by sleeping and slept by weeping and called out once. The words were dust. Who left late singing and signed up leaving and ran home slowly afraid of sleeping and hated thinking and thought by feeling and called out once but no one came,

who dreamt blue snow and froze in dreaming and spoke by reading and read all evening and read by patterns of blizzards drifting and dared by waiting and waited taking and called out once and called out twice and coughed grey clouds and carved four coffins and took by thanking and thanked by seeking and drifted bedwards and lay there weeping and counted her tears and divided by seven and called out once. The words were crows.

A Discourse on Optics

i. The Heirloom

Now its silver paint is flaking off,
That full-length antique bevelled mirror
Wants to be clear water in a trough,
Still, astringent water in November.

It worked for sixty years, day and night
Becoming this room and its passing faces.
Holding it now against the light
I see the sun shines through in places.

It wants to be the window that it was,
Invisible as pleasure or pain,
Framing whatever the day may cause –
The moon. A face. Rain.

I'll prop it up outside against the skip
So clouds can ghost across the rust.
Though I can't see myself in it,
Still, it's the only mirror that I trust.

ii. The Pond

The shape of man, a shadow on the ground,
Returns, a mirror image, from pondwater.
So it is we think the soul not shade,
Not silhouette, but solid matter.

Except those times light strikes the basin level
And almost makes a window of the surface
To show our shadow amid coins and gravel
Outgazing the sad overcoat and face,

To teach them, I suppose, they are that darkness
Deepening the bottom of the pool,
And teach the soul it wears the face and coat
Which that lucidity obscures.

II. O'Ryan's Belt

The Hunter's Purse

is the last unshattered 78
by 'Patrolman Jack O'Ryan, violin',
a Sligo fiddler in dry America.

A legend, he played Manhattan's ceilidhs,
fell asleep drunk one snowy Christmas
on a Central Park bench and froze solid.
They shipped his corpse home, like his records.

This record's record is its lunar surface.
I wouldn't risk my stylus to this gouge,
or this crater left by a flick of ash –

When Anne Quinn got hold of it back in Kilrush,
she took her fiddle to her shoulder
and cranked the new Horn of Plenty
Victrola over and over and over,
and scratched along until she had it right
or until her father shouted

> 'We'll have *no* more
> Of *that* tune
> In *this* house to*night*.'

She slipped out back and strapped the contraption
to the parcel rack and rode her bike
to a far field, by moonlight.

It skips. The penny I used for ballast slips.
O'Ryan's fiddle pops, and hiccoughs
back to this, back to this, back to this:
a napping snowman with a fiddlecase;
a flask of bootleg under his belt;
three stars; a gramophone on a pushbike;
a cigarette's glow from a far field;
over and over, three bars in common time.

A Repertoire

'Play us one we've never heard before'
we'd ask this old guy in our neighborhood.
He'd rosin up a good three or four
seconds, stalling, but he always could.
This was the Bronx in 1971,
when every night the sky was pink with arson.
He ran a bar beneath the el, the Blarney Stone,
and there one Easter day he sat us down
and made us tape as much as he could play;
'I gave you these. Make sure you put that down',
meaning all he didn't have to say.

All that summer we slept on fire escapes,
or tried to sleep, while sirens or the brass
from our neighbour's Tito Puente tapes
kept us up and made us late for Mass.
I found our back door bent back to admit
beneath the thick sweet reek of grass
a nest of needles, bottle caps, and shit.
By August Tom had sold the Blarney Stone
to Puerto Ricans, paid his debts in cash
but left enough to fly his body home.

The bar still rises from the South Bronx ash,
its yellow neon buzzing in the noonday
dark beneath the el, a sheet-steel door
bolted where he played each second Sunday.
'Play me one I've never heard before'
I'd say, and whether he recalled those notes
or made them up, or – since it was Tom who played –
whether it was something in his blood
(cancer, and he was childless and afraid)
I couldn't tell you. And he always would.

A Reprieve

'Realizing that few of the many tunes remembered from boyhood days . . . were
known to the galaxy of Irish musicians domiciled in Chicago, the writer
decided to have them preserved in musical notation. This was the initial step in
a congenial work which has filled in the interludes of a busy and eventful life.'

– Police Chief Francis O'Neill, *Irish Folk Music: A Fascinating Hobby,
with some Account of Related Subjects* (Chicago 1910)

Here in Chicago it's almost dawn
and quiet in the cell in Deering Street stationhouse
apart from the first birds at the window and the milkwagon
and the soft slap of the club in Chief O'Neill's palm.
'Think it over,' he says, 'but don't take all day.'
Nolan's hands are brown with a Chinaman's blood.
But if he agrees to play three jigs
slowly, so O'Neill can take them down,
he can walk home, change clothes,
and disappear past the stockyards and across the tracks.

Indiana is waiting. O'Neill lowers his eyes,
knowing the Chinaman's face will heal, the Great Lakes
roll in their cold grey sheets and wake,
picket lines will be charged, girls raped
in the sweatshops, the clapboard tenements burn.
And he knows that Nolan will be gone by then,
the coppery stains wiped from the keys of the blackwood flute.

Five thousand miles away Connaught sleeps.
The coast lights dwindle out along the west.
But there's music here in this lamplit cell,
and O'Neill scratching in his manuscript like a monk
at his illuminations, and Nolan's sweet tone breaking
as he tries to phrase a jig the same way twice:
'The Limerick Rake' or 'Tell her I am' or 'My Darling Asleep'.

Theodora, Theodora

Tomorrow, Parnassus. Tonight, outside the taverna,
you wait in the darkened coach alone
flaking *kif* into a roll-up by the dashboard light.
Plates crash. The band risk a verse or two
of a song they played before the war in brothels
where you fucked, gambled, and somehow failed
to die; a song about a girl who didn't.
For love. Slum music. Knives and despair.
Softly you sing what words you can remember.

There are stars in the chorus, and two brothers,
hashish, wisteria, a straight razor. You can't recall
the name of the song or the name of the girl
who bleeds to death at dawn by birdsong before the basilica,
but they're the same. It's been so long.
The bishops banned it, and the colonels,
and somehow even you – how else could you forget –
because these songs have backstreets much like this.
Bile and retsina. Streets the cops don't like.

Sixteen bars then into *Zorba*. The tour-group clap,
snap pictures, then stumble on board laughing
in accents of Buenos Aires or Chicago,
where coach drivers wait outside bars on the south side,
singing softly, for no one but themselves tonight,
of girls who bleed for love. 'Theodora.'
You remember. 'Theodora.' Singing too loud,
you take the slow road back to the hotel.

Down

The stars are shuffling slowly round
Burning in the dark
Upon the lips of angry men
Drinking in the park.
Five thousand fed. I read it in
The Gospel of St Mark.

Helicopters insect round
Above the burned-out cars.
Here where Gospel testified
Between the wars
His harp of darkness cried and prayed
To bottleneck guitars.

Tell me why's you cryin' baby?
I sure would like to know.
Tell me why's you cryin' baby?
I sure would like to know.
Some words I can't make out, and then,
I'll come walkin' through that door.

These flattened thirds and sevenths
Justified the Blues:
Intervals ruled by celestial laws,
Horse, and booze.
Woke up this morning's just the kind
Of line he couldn't use.

Cicadas carve across this night
Their lapidary phrase,
And the darkness children fear
They continually praise.
The darkness children fear, they
Continually praise.

The Classics

I remember it like it was last night,
Chicago, the back room of Flanagan's
malignant with accordions and cigarettes,
Joe Cooley bent above his Paolo Soprani,
its asthmatic bellows pumping as if to revive
the half-corpse strapped about it.
It's five a.m. Everyone's packed up.
His brother Seamus grabs Joe's elbow mid-arpeggio.
'Wake up, man. We have to catch a train.'
His eyelids fluttering, opening. The astonishment . . .

I saw this happen. Or heard it told so well
I've staged the whole drunk memory:
What does it matter now? It's ancient history.
Who can name them? Where lie their bones and armour?

III. True

The Chamber of Errors

It never gets as crowded as Tussaud's,
But every day we draw the curious few
Who've seen our sticker on the underground,
Our card in a phone box, and felt
That, somehow, it was printed just for them.
Of course, it was. Step in and look around.
You haven't come for Marilyn or Elvis.
Like you, I loathe that taxidermal bathos.
We use the faces left in photobooths
By rushed commuters. Their eyes already closed,
We only have to make them *look* like wax.

Now look you on the unfamiliar dead.
More than the pancaked meat in satin caskets,
More than the unforgiving memories,
These are your unforgiven. But be warned,
Like faces glimpsed in fever on the curtains,
These will never truly go away.
Look round, and after, should you need to rest,
And many do, there is a chesterfield.
But please, please, this is important,

Don't touch. I spend my life repairing details.
See where I've pressed the hairs in one by one?
And here? See where I've whorled the fingerpads?
I can't think what possesses people. *Christ*,
Sometimes, at night, I find the faces gouged.

Reliquary

The robot camera enters the *Titanic*
And we see her fish-cold nurseries on the news;
The toys of Pompeii trampled in the panic;
The death camp barrel of babyshoes;

The snow that covered up the lost girl's tracks;
The scapular she wore about her neck;
The broken doll the photojournalist packs
To toss into the foreground of the wreck.

Ovation

O pilgrim from above led through these flames,
There was a time I looked down on a thousand torches.

My voice brought such an echo of applause
You'd think each word a stone dropped in a well.

Our Land. Splash. *Justice long denied.*
Splash. *The humble exalted,*

The exalted . . . and so forth. Immortal words.
It was like love. And my queen loved me,
Could quote my book verbatim.

Then that winter underground, and the golden dream
Defiled by weaklings whispering like burning fat.
Even she was heard to whisper, my Isolde.

I hanged the astrologer, and slipped beneath my tongue
The key to the drawer in which lay locked
The cyanide, the Luger, and my speeches . . .

She would ridicule me in the end,
Quoting them to me verbatim.

Co-Pilot

He leadeth me in the paths of righteousness,
Sitting on my shoulder like a pirate's parrot,
Whispering the Decalogue like a tiny Charlton Heston.
Tch, he goes. *Tch Tch*. He boreth me spitless.

Tonight I need a party with a bottomless punchbowl
Brimming cool vodka to the lip of the horizon.
I'll yank him from his perch and hold him under
Until the bubbles stop.

Cage,

The composer, locked in a soundproof room in Harvard
Heard his heartbeat and the sound of Niagara Falls
Produced by the operation of his nervous system,
From which he derived a theory, no doubt.

Me, I heard a throaty click at the end of 'wedlock'.
And Niagara on the long-distance line.
I knew a couple once, went up there on their honeymoon.
After a week, they said, you don't even hear it.

Meridian

There are two kinds of people in the world.
Roughly. First there are the kind who say
'There are two kinds of people in the world'
And then there's those who don't.

Me, I live smack on the borderline,
Where the road ends with towers and searchlights,
And we're kept awake all night by the creak of the barrier
Rising and falling like Occam's razor.

Lives of the Artists

I. *The Age of Criticism*

The clergy, who are prone to vertigo,
Dictate to heaven with a megaphone.
And those addressing Michelangelo
As he was freeing David from the stone
As much as said they thought the nose too big.
He waited till he got them on their own,
Scooped some marble dust up with his tools,
And climbing loftily atop his rig,
He tapped his chisel for those squinting fools
And let a little dust fall on their faces.

He tapped and tapped. And nothing slowly changed
Except for the opinions of Their Graces.

II. *The Discovery and Loss of Perspective*

Her personal vanishing point,
she said, came when she leant
against his study door
all warm and wet and whispered
'Paolo. Bed.'

He only muttered,
gazing down his grid, 'Oh,
what a lovely thing perspective is!'
She went to live
with cousins in Madrid.

III. *The Advance of Naturalism*

As any dripping clepsydra, batsqueak
In the eaves, or square of angry birds,
So Donatello's steady chisel rhythm
Could sound like words. Perhaps you've read
How someone put his ear against a crack
And heard him try to make a statue speak.
Well, I was there. I heard it answer back.

Of all the cheek! it said, *Show some respect!*
The hand that makes us perfect makes us each
Submissive to the other's intellect.
Nor have we any confidence to teach
Through speaking sculpture or through sculptured speech.

Signifyin' Monkey

'Never write a check with your mouth your ass can't cash.'
                                            – Zach Newton

O.K. I'll tell it, but only if you buy lunch.
One summer I worked nights for Vigil-Guard,
the Chicago security firm. The work was easy:
sitting. And close to home. Ten minutes on the train.
And every night I passed the same fluorescent sign
somewhere in Chinatown: FIGHTER MONKEY.

I paid it no mind. It was the year of the monkey.
I thought I'd try it out one day for lunch.
Risky, I figured, but it's always a good sign
if the sign's in English. I wasn't made chief guard
for nothing, you know. It takes a week to train
on half pay so don't think it's all that easy.
Security's an art. I just make it *look* easy,
like the day I walked home past Fighter Monkey.
Looking back, I wish I'd caught that train,
but I was after a cheap pork feng shui lunch.
Something out front put me on my guard,
though, something about that Day-Glo sign,
the smell, and the cages in the windows, and no sign
of a menu anywhere, which made me a little uneasy,
when out steps this white guy built like a bodyguard
wearing a T-shirt showing a shrieking monkey.
He just stands there, chin out. 'Still serving lunch?'
I ask. 'This is no restaurant,' he says. 'I train
animals' – He's got this tight whisper – 'I train
Barbary Apes using American Sign
Language.' O.K. I figure he's out to lunch,
a potential situation. 'Take it easy,'
I tell him. 'I made a mistake. *You* train monkeys . . .
I represent a firm called Vigil-Guard.'

Turns out he once trained dogs for Vigil-Guard.
And he pays me there and then to help him train
one of his babies, a kind of Rottweiler monkey
that took her orders and talked back in Sign.
I swear she must have weighed forty pounds easy.
And teeth! She could have had me for lunch.
Shit, she could have had me *and* lunch!
Then he hauls out this heavy, padded armguard.
'Put that on,' he says. 'This part is safe and easy.
She's going to come at you like a freight train.
Freeze.' I remember he laughed as he made the sign.
The asshole. Lost a thumb to his own monkey.

It's easy. Look, he'd been her only trainer.
Guard or no guard, he'd signed 'I'm lunch.'
The blood! Of course they had to shoot the monkey.

Shooting *The Crane People*

It was a hard year and it was always raining.
The first six months they ran at our approach.
But finally, by patience and cunning,
we gained their trust. Or they learned to ignore us.

Their dialect is noisy and almost unlearnable.
There are no vowels. Their name for themselves,
for example, is a hiss followed by a tiny choking sound
and means 'we', but homophones abound.

Their name for us, a sharp intake of breath,
is also the word for mudslides, or a large, inedible carcass.
We found pronunciation difficult and the slightest error
was met with confusion, irritation, and contempt.

Though excellent telegenic material,
they couldn't recognize themselves on screen.
They move like cranes, and when they squat to dig for grubs
it's like the start of a sad slow dance.

They found our camera terrifying
and were eager to learn to use it.
Our guide would video his wives to punish them.
It was a hard year. I didn't like them. It was always raining.

Banzai

'Don't be nervous. Be hungry.'
Donovan refilled my *sake*.

The chairman was taller than I expected.
He sat at the head of the table,
Donovan between us to translate.

Looking at Donovan, he spoke to me
of risks, profits and futures, and
when Donovan crossed his fingers and winked,
I made my move, surprising myself.
'Tell him I want a taste of power.'
Donovan frowned with the effort.

A chrysanthemum pattern of glassy flesh
arrived which the chairman had ordered for us,
with gravity, several lifetimes earlier –
an expensive, mildly neurotoxic sashimi,
prepared by licensed chefs. Occasionally fatal.
He pincered a morsel, blinked, and swallowed.
Slainte he said, speaking to Donovan, looking at me.

Becoming Catastrophic

Purification itself takes several days. It is agonizing: explosive diarrhoea, sweats, retching, shaking, itching, freezing. But by the second morning the flesh turns white and gradually transparent. Fat, hair, and muscle are the last to go, until finally the tough black dots of the pupils wink out and you see through the world's eyes at last. This is why, having never been corporeal, Thrones, Principalities, Dominions and Powers cannot be depicted except as fortuitous events. Mate in five moves, say. And this is why, once invisible, pains must be taken to think invisibly, for to look too greenly on some sunlit apple's green ebullience can spark a plebiscite, freak hail, sunshower. Remember you are not omnipresent, only infinitely responsible. Always eat alone; your unassimilated food and waste may be visible for hours.

True

n 7 (as of a compass bearing) according to the earth's geographical rather than magnetic poles. True north.
vb 15 (tr) to adjust so as to make true.

i. A grand magic lantern entertainment

ONE NIGHT ONLY

illustrated by over FORTY DISSOLVENT VIEWS of a strictly moral character. Nothing to offend the most fastidious person.

Scriptural Views   Comic Songs and Speeches
Lord Franklin setting out to discover a northwest passage

AROUND THE POLE!

The Esquimeaux of the Labradors are aboriginals with no religious rite. Instead they catch beneath the ice a small, somewhat poisonous silver fish which they consume uncooked. This practice induces fever and vivid dreams, and they prognosticate by reading in the putrified viscera of seals.

Lord Franklin has just read 'Ulysses',
Tennyson's latest, and collapses
his brass collapsible telescope.

> *Twas homeward bound one night on the deep*
> *Swinging in my hammock I fell asleep.*
> *I dreamt a dream and I thought it true*
> *Concerning Franklin and his gallant crew.*

In June, becalmed in sight of a Swedish whaler,
Lord Franklin signalled her captain
to dinner followed by a game of backgammon.
But the long day waned and the sails filled,
and the English waved from the deck
till they were out of sight.
Old age hath yet its honour and its toil.

'One of our visitors held a pocketwatch to his ear. Supposing it to be alive, he asked if it was good to eat. Another, handed a wineglass, appeared very much astonished that it did not melt in the heat of his hand as he entertained a notion that it was made of ice.'

ii. Franklin missing

With a hundred seamen he sailed away
On the frozen ocean in the month of May.
In Baffin Bay where the whale fish below
The fate of Franklin no man may know.

'With interest which accumulates by the hour do we watch for the return of these two vessels which are perhaps even now working their way through the Bering Strait into the Pacific.'

The Sikh boy dims
a fringed gas lamp.
Mme Murphy, the sensitive,
bids Lady Franklin sit.

'Please join hands and empty your minds
of all worldly thoughts.'
She summons the spirit
of Sir John Franklin.

Silence in the perfumed dark.
The carriage clock needs winding.

Swedenborg, she explains,
holds that angels,
being purely selfless beings,
generate rather than take up space.
Jammed wing to wing, the halls of heaven
are vast and empty as the ice pack.

Someone coughs and fidgets.
'Wait . . . I see . . . I see . . .
No more today. Please. The palpitations.
Fetch the ladies' coats, Mahapatra,
and show Lord Merryll in.'

iii. The search party

And now my burden it gives me pain
To think my Franklin lies across the Main.
Ten thousand pounds would I freely give
To say on earth that my Franklin does live.

'We pressed on and discovered at four o clock
two skeletons in furs face down in the ice.
We scattered black matchstick bones
from one braided sleeve and found they'd clutched
a toothbrush and a silver medal for navigation
awarded by the Royal Naval College, 1830,
and the remains of a letter of which was legible:

". . . all spoilt. Seven hundred tins in all. Several strong men fainted
and wee drew lots to put out with . . . the long boat to look for free
wather. On the 12th night of our hawl, brother Dick, wee saw 2 very
large hice Burgh to windward of ous and we stopt in thare shadow for
to rest in the boat for the wether was bad and weed be out of the wind.
Apon taking off his boots wee see Capten Hughs has no payne in his
feet and says they feel warm but wee feer he will soon loose them. We
are most blynded from the hice and I feer, dear friends, I canot rite very
longer for my eyes hurt full sore and I am week for want of food. Tell
mother I die a Chrischun in Gods mercee

> Good by untell we meet in heven,
> Tom Cook"

For what we found next I regret I can offer
neither explanation nor conjecture,
for we discovered scattered about beneath half-buried sledges
seventy silk handkerchiefs, five pocket watches,
a badminton racket, a birdcage, a tiny clockwork cricket,
a brass telescope, and several barrel organs,
their gearwork still in fair condition.
One of these last I tested, and winding its handle
I succeeded in producing a medley from popular operettas
until a storm blew up and we struck back for camp.'

Privacy

Here, as in life, they were admitted
to a club exclusive as the Garrick,
now a kind of Victorian Angkor Wat
adjacent to the A road.
Their mossed, sepulchral pieties
neglected for decades, swallowed
back into a mild jungle,
their shapeless sculpture decked
flat, sprayed with uncouth rhymes,
their eminent corpses
violated by ritual necrophilia in the 60s,
how fares it with the happy dead?

The PM urges their revival,
the spirits of industry, exploration,
eels and gin, the floorless jig.
Here, everyone knows his place.
Here, little green bronze bells
festoon the exterior of the 'Egyptian' mausoleum.
The strings once led inside,
where, waking in their two inch dark,
the prematurely interred
could tintinnabulate as if for tea.
Sadly, these have snapped.

The Raindial

The sun goes in. The light goes out.
A million shadows fade away.
It could be any time of day.
Now dream that you don't dream about
The garden of this Hackney squat
Where dark drops stipple on the *Sun*,
The umbrella skeleton,
The sink, the broken flowerpot . . .

A cold rain slicks the garden path
That leads you down the overgrowth
Toward the monument to Thoth:
A drowned shark in a birdbath.

Above its fin the zodiac
Spins upon its sentinel.
The gnomon knows, but will not tell
The time nor give your future back.
The gnomon knows. And round it's writ
As these long   pass swift away
So too the hope of man decays.
TippExed under pigeonshit,
The years, the months, the weeks, the days.

The Brother

Dropping a canapé in my Beaujolais
At some reception, opening or launch,
I recall briefly the brother I never had
Presiding at less worldly rituals:
The only man at my wedding not wearing a tie;
Avuncular, swaddling my nephew over the font;
Thumbing cool oil on our mother's forehead
In the darkened room, the bells and frankincense . . .
While the prodigal sweats in the strip-lit corridor.

Now, picture us facing each other, myself and the brother
I never met: two profiles in silhouette,
Or else a chalice, depending how you look.
Imagine that's this polystyrene cup.
I must break bread with my own flesh and blood.

Fraction

The fourteenth time my mother told the story
Of her cousins dismembered by a British bomb,
I turned on her, her Irish son. 'I'm American.
I was born here.' She went to pieces.

And would not be solaced. I had her eyes,
The aunt's, that is, who, the story goes,
Was brought to the jail to sort the bits in tubs.
Toes. I meant to renounce such grotesque pity.

I was thirteen. I didn't know who I was. She knew.
As I held her wrists, reassuring,
Repeating, that I was her Irish son,
I was the man who'd clicked the toggle switch

Bracing himself between two branches,
Between the flash and the report.

Erratum

I touch the cold flesh of a god in the V and A,
the guard asleep in his chair, and I'm shocked
to find it's plaster. These are the reproduction rooms,
where the David stands side by side with the Moses
and Trajan's column (in two halves).
It reminds me of the inventory sequence in *Citizen Kane*.
It reminds me of an evening twenty years ago.

And all at once I'm there, at her side,
turning the pages as she plays
from the yellowed song sheets I rescued from a bookstall:
Dodd's setting of *Antony and Cleopatra*. All very improving.
'Give me my robe and crown,' she warbles
in a Victorian coloratura. 'I have immoral longings in me.'

I want to correct her – the word on the page is
immortal – but I'm fourteen and scandalized.
(I knew there were no innocent mistakes.
I'd finished *Modern Masters: Freud*
before she snatched and burned it. 'Filth' –
yanking each signature free of the spine,
'Filth. Filth. Filth.')

The song is over. But when she smiles at me,
I'm on the verge of tears, staring down at the gap-
toothed grimace of our old Bechstein. 'What's wrong?'
What's *wrong*? I check the word again. She's right. Immoral.
She shows me the printer's slip, infecting
the back page of every copy, like,
she might have said, the first sin.

The guard snorts in his dream. I take my palm away
still cool from what I'd taken to be marble.
And when I get that moment back, it's later;
I'm sobbing on her shoulder and I can't say why.
So she suggests another visit to the furnace, where,
to comfort me, perhaps, we rake the cinders with the music
till they chink and spark, and shove the pages
straight to the white core to watch them darken as if ageing,
blacken, enfold, like a sped-up film of blossoms in reverse.

Some Notes

The Hunter's Purse – 'Well, they used to come by emigrants coming home on holidays, mostly, because they'd imagine if they posted them they'd be broken, which they would at the time. And it was all returned Americans coming home to see their own native place again that brought both the gramophones and the records. And there was as much lookout for an emigrant returning home that time as there would be for – I don't know what now, to see an aeroplane going into orbit or something off the ground. Because there was an awful lookout for John McKenna's records, an awful lookout.' – Tommy Gilmartin, quoted by Harry Bradshaw and Jackie Small in 'John McKenna, Leitrim's master of the Concert flute' (*Musical Traditions*, No. 7, 1987).

A Repertoire – 'Play me one we've never heard before.' Chicago fiddler Liz Carroll would ask this of the late Johnny McGreevy who would alway comply. But the poem is not about Johnny.

Theodora, Theodora – In 'The Gangster Reformed, A study in musical parallels' Jaoa Dos Santos compares the subcultures of Tango, Fado, and Rembetika (*Musical Traditions*, No. 7, 1987). He might also consider the lifespan of urban Blues.

Down – What I heard of the song was sung by Jimmy Reed.

Lives of the Artists – Three misremembered episodes from Vasari's lives of, respectively, Michelangelo, Uccello, and Donatello. He remarks that the latter used to mutter to his favourite piece, the *Zuccone*, 'Speak, or the plague take you!'

Signifyin' Monkey – is the title of an R&B standard. Vigil-Guard were a private security firm on Chicago's west side. Zach Newton was my supervisor there.

Banzai – *Fugu* (*Canthigaster riulatus, Fugu rubripes* or Pacific pufferfish), if improperly filleted of its liver and roe, causes paralysis and death within minutes.

True – Most of it is. The song is a Victorian broadside I got from the singing of Micheal O'Domhnaill. Some of the other quotations are from Ross, Captain John, *A Voyage of Discovery in HM Ships 'Isabella and Alexander'* (John Murray, 1819) and Lord Egerton in the *London Quarterly Review* (June 1847), which is quoted in Evan S. Connell's account of the Franklin expedition in *A Long Desire* (Holt Reinhart and Winston, 1977). Other quotations are trued.

CONJURE

for Ruairí Tomás,

HORATIO: It beckons you to go away with it
As if it some impartment did desire
To you alone

Only me, old son.

Contents

The Excuse

Please hang up. I try again.
'My father's sudden death has shocked us all'
Even me, and I've just made it up,
Like the puncture, the cheque in the post,
Or my realistic cough. As I'm believed,
I'm off the hook. But something snags and holds.

My people were magicians. Home from school,
I followed a wire beneath the table to
A doorbell. I rang it. My father looked up.

Son, when your uncle gets me on the phone
He won't let go. I had to rig up something.

Midnight. I pick up and there's no one there,
No one, invoked, beyond that drone. But if
I had to rig up something, and I do,
Let my excuse be this, and this is true:
I fear for him and grieve him more than any,
This most deceiving and deceived of men . . .
Please hang up and try again.

Not Knowing the Words

Before he wearied of the task, he sang a nightly Mass
for the repose of the souls of the faithful departed
and magicked his blood to bourbon and tears
over the ring, the lock of hair, the dry pink dentures.
Was he talking to her? I never learned.
Walk in, he'd pretend to be humming softly,
like wind through a window frame.

The last I saw of him alive, he pressed me to his coat.
It stinks in a sack in my attic like a drowned Alsatian.
It's his silence. Am I talking to him now, as I get it out
and pull its damp night down about my shoulders?
Shall I take up the task, and fill its tweedy skin?
Do I stand here not knowing the words
when someone walks in?

Caliban's Books

Hair oil, boiled sweets, chalk dust, squid's ink . . .
Bear with me. I'm trying to conjure my father,
age fourteen, as Caliban – picked by Mr Quinn
for the role he was born to play because
'I was the handsomest boy at school'
he'll say, straight-faced, at fifty.
This isn't easy. I've only half the spell,
and I won't be born for twenty years.
I'm trying for rainlight on Belfast Lough
and listening for a small, blunt accent
barking over the hiss of a stove getting louder like surf.
But how can I read when the schoolroom's gone
black as the hold of a ship? Start again.

Hair oil, boiled sweets . . .
But his paperbacks are crumbling in my hands,
seachanged bouquets, each brown page
scribbled on, underlined, memorized,
forgotten like used pornography:
The Pocket Treasury of English Verse,
How to Win Friends and Influence People,
Thirty Days To a More Powerful Vocabulary.

Fish stink, pitch stink, seaspray, cedarwood . . .
I seem to have brought us to the port of Naples,
midnight, to a shadow below deck
dreaming of a distant island.
So many years, so many ports ago!
The moment comes. It slips from the hold
and knucklewalks across the dark piazza
sobbing *maestro! maestro!* But the duke's long dead
and all his magic books are drowned.

Black Ice and Rain

Psalms 6.6

Can I come in? I saw you slip away.
Hors d'oeuvres depress you, don't they? They do me.
And cocktails, jokes . . . such dutiful abandon.
Where the faithful observe immovable feasts
– boat races, birthdays, marriages, martyrdoms –
we're summoned to our lonely ceremonies any time:
B minor, the mouldiness of an old encyclopedia,
the tinny sun snapping off the playground swings,
these are, though we can't know this, scheduled
to arrive that minute of the hour, hour of the day,
day of every year. Again, regular as brickwork,
comes the time the nurse jots on your chart
before she pulls the sheet across your face. Just so,
the past falls open anywhere – even sitting here with you.

Sorry. You remind me of a girl I knew.
I met her at a party much like this, but younger, louder,
the bass so fat, the night so sticky you could drown.
We shouted art at each other over soul
and cold beer in the crowded kitchen and I, at least,
was halfway to a kiss when she slipped
her arm around her friend.
I worked at liking him, and it took work,
and it never got any easier being harmless,
but we danced that night like a three-way game of chess
and sang to Curtis Mayfield pumped so loud
that when I drove them home they could hardly
whisper to invite me up.

Their black walls smirked with Jesus on black velvet
– Jesus, Elvis, Mexican skeletons, big-eyed Virgins,
Rodin's hands clasped in chocolate prayer –
an attitude of decor, not like this room of yours.
A bottle opened – tequila with a cringe of worm –
and she watched me.
Lighting a meltdown of Paschal candles,
she watched me. He poured the drinks rasping
We're seriously into cultural detritus. At which, at last,
she smiled. Ice cubes cracked. The worm sank in my glass.
And all that long year we were joined at the hip.

I never heard them laugh. They had,
instead, this tic of scratching quotes in air –
like frightened mimes inside their box of style,
that first class carriage from whose bright window
I watched the suburbs of my life recede.
        Exactly one year on she let me kiss her – once –
her mouth wine-chilled, my tongue a clumsy guest,
and after that the invitations dwindled.
By Christmas we were strangers. It was chance
I heard about the crash. He died at once.
Black ice and rain, they said. No news of her.

I can't remember why I didn't write.
Perhaps I thought she'd sold the flat and left.

Some nights midway to sleep I'm six years old.
Downstairs it's New Year's Eve. Drink and shrieks.
But my mother's lit the luminous plastic Jesus
to watch me through the night, which is why
I've got my pillow wrapped around my head.
I never hear the door. And when she speaks,
her thick-tongued anger rearing like a beast,
I feel my hot piss spreading through the sheets.
But when I wake, grown up, it's only sweat.
But if I dream, I bleed. A briar crown,
a fist prised open wide, a steadied nail,
a hammer swinging down – the past falls open
anywhere . . .

                    Ash Wednesday evening.
Driving by, I saw her lights were on.
I noticed both their names still on the buzzer
and when I rang I heard her voice. *Come in* –

        her nose was broken, her front teeth gone,
a rosary was twisted round her fists –

        – *Come in. I've been saying a novena.*
Inside, each crucifix and candle shone
transfigured in her chrysalis of grief.
She spoke about the crash, how she'd been driving,
how they had to cut her from the wreck . . .
and then she slipped and called me by his name.

Of those next hours I remember most
the silences between her sobs, the rain
against the skylight slowly weakening
to silence, silence brimming into sleep and dawn.
Then, having lain at last all night beside her,
having searched at last that black-walled room,
the last unopened chamber of my heart,
and found there neither pity nor desire
but an assortment of religious kitsch,
I inched my arm from under her and left.

     Since then, the calmest voice contains her cry
just within the range of human hearing
and where I've hoped to hear my name gasped out
from cradle, love bed, death bed, there instead
I catch her voice, her broken lisp, his name.
Since then, each night contains all others,
nested mirror-within-mirror, stretching back from then
to here and now, this party, this room, this bed,
where, in another life, we might have kissed.
Thank you, friend, for showing me your things –
you have exquisite taste – but let's rejoin your guests
who must by now be wondering where you've gone.

Our Life Stories

What did they call that ball in *Citizen Kane*?
That crystal blizzardball forecasting his past?
Surely I know the name. Your mum's souvenir
of Blackpool, underwater, in winter –
say we dropped it. What would we say we broke?
And see what it says when you turn it over . . .

I dreamt the little Christmas dome I owned
slipped my soapy fingers and exploded.
Baby Jesus and the Virgin Mother
twitching on the lino like dying guppies.
Let's shake this up and change the weather.

Catch! This marvellous drop, like its own tear,
has leaked for years. The tiny Ferris wheel has surfaced
in an oval bubble where it never snows
and little by little all is forgotten. Shhh!
Let's hold the sad toy storms in which we're held,
let's hold them gingerly above the bed,
bubbles gulping contentedly, as we rock them to sleep,
flurries aswim by our gentle skill,
their names on the tips of our tongues.

Duffel coat. Tennents Extra. No dog.

The rage has eaten the soft of his face away.
He starts to scream before his mouth can open,

screams as Jesus bellowed through the temple
dashing the tables of the dove-vendors and moneychangers,

as Achilles stood on the dyke and loosed the shout that kills,
felling twelve Trojans among their spears and chariots.

Window-rattling, spit-flecked, it peaks, cracks, subsides –
the cry from the tall grass at twilight

from the slow one, the straggler, run out by the herd,
outrun by the lioness.

The Tragedies

Upstage, spotlit, the prince soliloquizes
while courtiers ham their business in the dark.
We see you taking snuff, dim improvisers.
We won't remember, but you've left your mark
within the compass of our sense of sight.

It's how we speed down narrow streets and park.
It's how owls reconnoitre fields by night.

And dimmer, in the wings, the age grows vague
and greyly out of focus. Children die,
a page reports, in papal war and plague.
We glimpse them out the corner of our eye
and see them without looking, without pain.
We aim our minds like arrows at the Dane.

He dies. *Go bid the soldiers shoot.* Applause
like big wings flapping from an autumn field.
Now, as we glance about, the dark withdraws.
The stage dissolves. The orchestra's revealed
as though the light were rising on a tide
past stalls and circle to the streets outside,
as though the vision centred everywhere.

No animal eye can long survive that glare.

> *And let me speak to the yet unknowing world*
> *How these things came about.*
>   You caught its eye.
Its talons stretched. A silent wing unfurled.
A shadow glided gently from the sky.

My Flu

I'd swear blind it's June, 1962.
Oswald's back from Minsk. U2s glide over Cuba.
My cousin's in Saigon. My father's in bed
with my mother. I'm eight and in bed with my flu.
I'd *swear*, but I can't be recalling this sharp reek of Vicks,
the bedroom's fevered wallpaper, the neighbour's TV,
the rain, the tyres' hiss through rain, the rain smell.
This would never stand up in court – I'm asleep.

I'm curled up, shivering, fighting to wake,
but I can't turn my face from the pit in the woods
– snow filling the broken suitcases, a boy curled up,
like me, as if asleep, except he has no eyes.
One of my father's stories from the war
has got behind my face and filmed itself:
the village written off the map, its only witnesses
marched to the trees. Now all the birds fly up at once.

And who filmed *this* for us, a boy asleep in 1962,
his long-forgotten room, his flu, this endless rain,
the skewed fan rattling, the shouts next door?
My fever reaches 104. But suddenly he's here,
I'd swear, all round me, his hand beneath my head
until one world rings truer than the other.

The Palm

la connaissance aux cent passages

– René Char

That motorcycle downstairs never starts
but, like a statue with a stomach flu,
disturbs him with its monumental farts.
His phone won't stop. His arts review is due
and must be in the post by half past three
to make this issue of *Je Suis Partout*.
And here's another *merde* to fuel his rage:
he has to wrestle with a rusty key.
Though they assured him this machine was new,
he's got to press the 'j' against the page
whenever he types *jazz* or *Juiverie*
and he uses these words frequently.
It jams again, the phone rings. Bang on cue,
the motorcycle starts. The curtains part
on the Palm Casino, 1942.

> Although he thinks she's buying out the town
> the critic's wife sits on an unmade bed
> in room 6, naked, as her palm is read
> by a guitarist in a dressing gown.
> He reels off lines in the forgotten script
> that maps her palm: *Here is your first affair* . . .
> He looks at her but she can't help but stare
> down at the hand in which her hand is gripped.

Rethinking his title, 'For the Masses',
typewriter underarm, the critic passes
in the hallway a trolley of caramelized pears
and a fat man with a string bass case who stares
suspiciously back behind dark glasses.
Could this be M. Vola, room 9, who plays
that nigger music for Vichy gourmets,
hunting the gypsy guitarist in his band?
The critic squints to memorize his face
as the lift cage rattles open for Vola and his bass.
Voilà! He'll call it 'Rhetoric and Race'.

But back to those pears. Glazed, tanned,
they fall in behind a whole roast pig
delivered to the gypsy's room before the gig.
He watches the waiter watch his crippled hand
as, with the other, he tries to sign his name.
He's new at this. It never looks the same.

The typewriter? Dismantled. All the keys
arranged across a workbench side by side.
And the critic hissing *Can I have your name please?*
and *What do you mean you're not qualified?*
and *Shall we call the police judiciaire?*
Tomorrow he will not be everywhere.

Tonight the gypsy counts in the Quintet.
They'll play until the curfew lifts at dawn.
They have to call this foxtrot 'La Soubrette'
but it's 'I've Got My Love To Keep Me Warm'.

Resolution

The new year blurs the windowpane.
Soho surrenders to the rain
as clouds break over Chinatown.
See how the storm's resolve winds down?
Its steel pins thin and mist away.
Get up. Come here and see the day.

Through this droplet's contact lens,
the West End and the future tense
look dainty, vacant, and convex.
We haven't seen such weather since
the morning they invented sex.
And yet, baptized, by rain and gin,
of last year's unoriginal sins
of inattention and cliché,
this looks like every other day
that we will never see again.

Courage. Coffee. Aspirins.
Our window on the world begins
to dry, the breakfast bulletins
appal, the civil voices lie,
our private garden cloud with doubt.
So let me make *this* crystal clear:
the rain has stopped. Your taxi's here.
The New Year bells will ring you out.

Refusals

Shooting their horses and setting their houses alight,
The faithful struck out for a hillside in Sussex
To wait for the prophesied rapture to take them
At midnight, New Year's Eve, 1899.

But they knelt in the slow, drifting snow singing hymns,
Hushing their children and watching the stars,
Until the sky brightened and the cold sun rose white
Over the plain where their houses still smouldered.

Some froze there all day, some straggled back sobbing
To salvage what little remained of their lives.
Others went mad and refused, till the end of their days,
To believe that the world was still there.

Here, ten seconds to midnight, they join in the count
Over tin horns squealing in the bright drunk rooms.

5:00/5:10/5:15

We shared a dream beneath
a dream-beneath-a-dream.
Our tears became a storm
that washed away our names
and our voices blended with the rain's.
Whatever does the singing sang
about, and then away, the pain
of having been
one creature torn in two.

Then whatever does the waking
woke, or dreamt it woke, to share
our dream-beneath-a-dream
before the primed alarm could tear
us back to me and you.

This is no dream: It's 5:15.
I wake. I pack. Before I go
I'll press my ear against your back –
a hostage at a wall – to hear
one beat. No. Two beats fall.

The Break

Like freak Texan sisters joined at the hip
playing saxophone duets in vaudeville,
we slept leaning, back to back.
When, more and more, our silences deepened,
a new perfume, a phone bill in her padlocked journal,
were props on a stage inside my head
where I woke sweat-drenched, alone.
Now she's gone, I seem to crowd myself because
it takes a second soul to hear the soul,
a third to hear the second . . . they keep coming:
angels many-armed, heraldic chimeras,
two-headed monsters at the map's edge screaming.

Inseparable sisters, I watch you every night
from my half-world, my single mattress.
You are smoking out back between shows
wearing the teal silk double cocktail dress.
You never speak. You pass the smoke,
and the silence between you is a lake on the moon.
Daisy, Violet, you are a girl at a dance
resting for a moment, against a mirror.

Celibates

They're closing down the travelling fair this week.
The crystal balls are packed, the last sword swallowed,
and the geek has shaved and caught the night bus home.
Beyond the dimming generator lights we stick it out,
blind masters of the dying arts, by night, by winter rain,
squatting in the rotting straw of our cages.
The recordreader strokes a disc and snaps back
Gould, *The French Suites*. The booksniffer naps,
face pressed to the uncut pages of the life of Keats
that he has just inhaled. The last haruspicator
snacks on hay with the phrenologist whilst I perform
another brilliant twist in the Mercan Variation
of the Queen's Gambit! History, made, fades away
unseen – as interest in exhibition solo chess
has markedly declined. But you, you inspire us,
frighten us, with your extraordinary abstinence,
obscurity and silence. Only a soft chittering
tells me you're there now, naked, knitting,
with tweezers, small flames – dark gold flash
of brass foil, spring coil, and gear – into tonight's
unsold array of clockwork crickets.

Reprimands

John 20: 24–29

We fell out of love as toddlers fall
glancing down, distracted, at their feet,
as the pianist in the concert hall
betrays her hands to thought and adds an extra
beat –
The thought vertiginous. The reprimand.
It fells the bee mid-flight. It made me stall
before a holy water font in Rome
half afraid that if I dipped my hand
I'd find the water's surface hard as stone
and – this you'd never understand –
half afraid to leave the thing alone.
For I'd been taught that Jesus walked the sea
and came to Peter three leagues out of port.
Said Peter *Bid me to come unto thee*
and strode on faith dryfoot until he thought . . .
and thinking, sank. I'd never learnt to swim
but I'd seen insects skim across a pond
and I'd seen glasses filled above the brim.
Some firm conviction keeps a raindrop round.
What kept me rigid as a mannequin?

We fell out of love and nearly drowned.
The very wordlessness all lovers want
to feel beneath their feet like solid ground
dissolved to silences no human shout
could ripple –
                        like the surface of that font
when other voices, tourist and devout,

grew still, and someone whispered by my side
O ye of little faith – and shallow doubt –
choose here to wet that hand or stand aside.
No one was there. But I could tell that tone.
I heard his ancient apostolic voice
this evening when I went to lift the phone
to tell you this – and froze. The reprimand.
For once, in two minds, Thomas made the choice
to bless and wet with blood his faithless hand.

The Drop

We taped it under the seats,
packed it into the door panels,
drove it over the mountains in July,
and the other two hadn't a word of the language
not a word, not *help*, not *food*,
and always that fear of the sirens and lights, until,
at the end, we drove all night screaming
our throats raw over the radio to keep awake,
words we didn't understand, *mi corazón*,
every other word, *mi corazón*, then,
an hour to dawn the day of the drop, we drove down
through Calvária – just hours to go, but
we turned off the road near a fairground to dodgems,
carousel, all boarded up, spent fires, an old starving bitch
limping loose through the trailers. To nothing.

We got out to piss then waited for dawn in the car.
After days on the road we were talked out, hoarse,
but this was different, I remember, I *think* I remember,
paint peeling on the hoardings, the sun floating up
red through the dust and mesquite smoke. Crows.
The place seemed emptied even of ourselves.
And then we drove on to the drop.

I'd forgotten, and you never asked . . .
But it all came back last night. Trouble outside –
a speeding siren woke me, tuning down a fifth,
and I realized I'd been dreaming of that morning,
the three of us sitting in the car and, somehow,
I was standing outside too, watching us. I couldn't speak
because I'd used up all the words.

But it was the words had used me up
and left me black birds, a white dog, and *corazón*.
But this was years ago. Years. Before I met you.
The money? It went where money goes.

Where is it written that I must end here,

incipit, a great gold foliate Q surrounding my garden wherein nuns fiddle, philosophers discourse on the augmented fourth, the $\sqrt{-1}$? A window opens, a wax cylinder crackles, and the castrato's trill is borne on the wind to the skating peasantry. Across the frozen lake two boys set fire to a cat; here, the first of thirteen bears in the Queen's bear garden, its eyes scooped out, its nose blown full of pepper, shakes two mastiffs from its back and bellows; the youngest barn burner to be hanged is eight. His parents are made to watch. Here, beyond the scaffold and the smoke, a distant hill. On the hill a windmill; in its engine room a desk; on the desk a psalter; scrawled in its margin a prayer in the shape of a conch; in that prayer a devil-snare wound in a spiral of words. I would be the demon seduced by the riddle, lost in the middle, who cannot read back.

from The Deadly Virtues

iv. Faith

Three hundred gathered at the Angel of the North.
The crowds looked up at Blackpool Pier.
The crowds looked up so they could tell their children's children
They'd witnessed the occlusion of his iris.
At noon, at more than a thousand miles an hour,
his shadow raced across the Channel and silenced the birds.
For a moment the predator's vertical pupil dilated
as his children raised their faces and returned, through tears,
through treated glass, through welders' masks,
the gaze they had avoided all their lives.

vii. Justice

She's invisible because she's blind.
She can't be ugly. She has no face.
She will check that each confession's signed
and weigh each individual case.
She has no tongue but the final word.
She has no body. She is everyone.
It is she who bears the scales, the sword,
and noose and cattle prod and gun.

Timing

Yes I know it's not funny. A prisoner told me
when I was an orderly during the war,
exactly the way that I told it, the whores and the mice.
I say told though I should say he gargled or grunted –
we'd built him a jaw out of one of his ribs
so it took him some time. When he got near the end
and my tunic was freckled with mucus and blood
and the mask of my face ached from grinning
he pulled me down close for the punch line.
He said it. I waited – the way that you waited just now –
but its door never opened.
                              I'm sure that was it,
word for word, though he had neither English nor lips,
because after I searched what remained of his face
he started the torture again. An infection, I reckoned,
and dabbed at his wound and returned to my rounds
but it buzzed round my head like a wasp. Was it code?
If he took me for one of his own in his fever
what might he betray? I ran back at first light
but he'd died in the night of pneumonia.

I'm sure there are those men who laugh out of etiquette,
bafflement, fear of appearing obtuse, or just fear,
and men who dismiss it, or lose it, or change it
before it begins to change them.
Only one in a thousand, perhaps, will remember,
exactly, repeat it, exactly the way that I tell it.
I knew when you hailed me tonight at the station,
I said to myself, as you climbed in the back, he's the one.

Irena of Alexandria

Creator, thank You for humbling me.
Creator, who twice empowered me to change
a jackal to a saucer of milk,
a cloud of gnats into a chandelier,
and once, before the emperor's astrologers,
a nice distinction into an accordion,
and back again, thank You
for choosing Irena to eclipse me.

She changed a loaf of bread into a loaf of bread,
caused a river to flow downstream,
left the leper to limp home grinning and leprous,
because, the bishops say, Your will burns
bright about her as a flame about a wick.

Thank You, Creator, for taking the crowds away.
Not even the blind come here now.
I have one bowl, a stream too cold to squat in,
and the patience of a saint. Peace be,
in the meantime, upon her. And youth.
May sparrows continue to litter her shoulders,
children carpet her footsteps in lavender,
and may her martyrdom be beautiful and slow.

A Nun's Story

i.m. N.C.

That's Timmy, with his eyes shut
in our class photo snapped by Diane Arbus
before her *Vogue* days. If he grew up,
he swore, he'd devote his life to God.
Sister Tim. He stole *A Nun's Story*
and acted out scenes from *Black Narcissus*
wearing the hood of his sweatshirt up,
habitually. We studied together
in his kitchen when we were ten.
Above the table hung icons of the Kennedys,
DeValera, and Tim's black-belt dad
splitting a plank with his bare foot.
We lost touch at fifteen, as if he'd entered
a silent order. Perhaps he has. But I think
Sister Tim chainsmokes. I think
he lives with a Cuban bodybuilder
in the East Village, having, like everyman
in his season, a true vocation.

Local 32B

(US National Union of Building Service Workers)

The rich are different. Where we have doorknobs,
they have doormen – like me, a cigar store Indian
on the Upper East Side, in polyester, in August.
As the tenants tanned in Tenerife and Monaco
I stood guard beneath Manhattan's leaden light
watching poodle turds bake grey in half an hour.
Another hot one, Mr Rockefeller!
An Irish doorman foresees his death,
waves, and runs to help it with its packages.
Once I got a cab for Pavarotti. No kidding.
No tip either. I stared after him down Fifth
and caught him looking after me, then through me,
like Samson, eyeless, at the Philistine chorus –
Yessir, I put the tenor in the vehicle.
And a mighty tight squeeze it was.

Regarding Our Late Correspondence

Often I'll begin to write to you
and find I'm simply copying the plot,
that glass machine that dictates what we do.
    And often I'll be chalking up a cue,
clocking each ball rolling towards its slot
in that web of vectors
        – and I'm *crap* –

But it's my balance makes me miss my shot;
balancing the angle of my aim
against the random factors of the nap,
    or point of impact, say, or force, or weight,
or the chance of having missed the game
or having turned up pissed,
        an hour late.

But like I said, I'm crap at games.
I know. We know we can't finesse what's been.
we only have that instant of our skill,
    to squint across a field of abstract green,
or print *forgive me* in unbroken script,
sharpening the focus of our will
on making what comes next be
        what we mean . . .

which is where my aim has always slipped,
as often, in the night, I freeze mid-dream.
Just before I wake and lose the drift,
    a soft *clack* startles me, I turn towards you,
a million miniature pistons shift
the spindly camshaft of a vast machine
beneath the rumbling as the last balls drop.
    As, often, I'll begin to write to you,
        and stop.

Tears

      are shed, and every day
workers recover
the bloated cadavers
of lovers or lover
who drown in cars this way.

And they crowbar the door
and ordinary stories pour,
furl, crash, and spill downhill –
as water will – not orient,
nor sparkling, but still

The River in Spate

       sweeps us both down its cold grey current.
Grey now as your father was when I met you,
I wake even now on that shore where once,
sweat slick and still, we breathed together –
in – soft rain gentling the level of the lake,
out – bright mist rising from the lake at dawn.
How long before we gave each other to sleep,
to air – drawing the mist up, exhaling the rain?
Though we fight now for breath and weaken
in the torrent's surge to the dark of its mouth,
you are still asleep in my arms by its source,
small waves lapping the gravel shore,
and I am still awake and watching you,
in wonder, without sadness, like a child.

The Pallace of Memoria garnished with
Perpetuall Shininge Glorious Lightes Innumerable

It's shut. And after such a climb!
A caustic drizzle slicks the deserted funicular railway
as the lights come on below in the abandoned weekend.
The distant band's just tuning up in the life you missed.
Your beloved dead are back there
getting dressed for their garden parties.
Yours was among the first families of Purgatory.

When you return now to your ancestral gardens
you hear always an orchestra distantly, carefully,
mimicking the rain, or the sobbing of your national bird.
When you enter the deserted manor
you are often met by the police, who recognize you, bow,
and torture you by weeping during their inquiries
as is the custom of your country.

Annie

Flicker, stranger. Flare and gutter out.
The life you fight for is the light you kept.
That task has passed this hour from wick to window.
Fade you among my dead my never-daughter.

Upriver in your mother's blood and mine
it's always night. Their kitchen windows burn
whom we can neither name nor say we loved.
Go to them and take this letter with you.

Go let them pick you up and dandle you
and sing you lullabies before the hob.

April 28th, 1940

the clear cold of it that morning this was nine
when the milkman's daughter had been sent round
that morning to show us her first communion dress
and I spilt tea on the linen and the stain
spread this was nine and my mother fussed over her
as the sirens started up the clear cold above
that morning the stain spread in the air sent round
that morning to show us her first communion dress
and bundled her out the door to run the few yards
home and the stain spread in the clear sky she was nine
when we crawled from the cellar that morning we found
our roof blown clean away to the clear cold above
on my bicycle down to see the smoking street and her house
gone to shingles and bricks and timber and armchairs and glass
and her father was sobbing and calling her name
and I looked in their garden to the white dress soaked
red to the waist and the stain spread

Needlework

tattoos commissioned for the
1999 'Last Words' poetry festival, Salisbury

i

Copy this across your heart,
Whisper what your eyes have heard,
To summon me when we're apart,
This word made flesh, this flesh made word.

ii

The serpent sheds her skin and yet
The pattern she'd as soon forget
Recalls itself. By this I swear
I am the sentence that I bare.

proportion

Who fit that sash in the back window? And
who took this snapshot of us at the airport,
tilting your camera woozily? Whose thumb
occludes us? Are we crying before this
stranger? Who saved it, creased it,
smoothed it, fixed it to black paper by four
right-angle triangles? No master framer
reckoning by golden section, no
journeyman riffling soft curls of cedar to
vines, cornets, *putti* and *fleurs de lys*. No.
Whoever fit that bastard sash out back
queered it at such a slant you've got to ram
the heel of your hand slam up against it –
good, white-glossed Protestant pine, plain
as the pane that rattles when it shuts

The Years

Penetrar el espejo, faceless gods,
Cagers of the heart's four crowded rooms,
Guardians of crossroads, breakers of locks,
Openers of tombs,
     Rise up rise up from the floor of this house
Up the veins of my leg like a riptide.
Darklings, listen, I am your last gamble.
I am bridled and saddled. Enter the stable.
I am yours to ride.

     When the windows slammed shut
Through the gang-raped summer
And meths-soaked rags ignited in the dives,
You held us down, defiler of dreams,
You struck the matches, you opened the knives.
     When the rivet shot
Through my father's boot
And he tracked bloody prints on the factory floor,
You threw him the mop, degrader of souls,
You made him clock out, you showed him the door.
     And when I lay awake
To the gargling drain
Or the curtain rippled sun across the wall,
You mopped my forehead, mother of whispers
You bathed me in sleep, you let the night fall.

     Pick up the phone. I'm alone on the corner.
Fill in my timesheet, I'll help you remember.
Peel my face from the glass, lift my foot from the brake,
Run the film backwards, rewind the tape.
     Penetrar el espejo, bastard powers
Of the brick through the window and the drunken kiss,
How could I put any one god before you?
How would I know any world but this?

Mine

How long is a piece of string?
I give it maybe twenty years. From my beginning
to his end, a cable jerks tight, sings, twists, and frays.
And if you enter, how will you get back?
But that's where you come in.
I'll be down there reeling out this line
behind me like a diver's air hose. Hold this.
I'll only be gone a moment.
How long is a moment?
A mile of eighteen-inch seam in anthracite,
six inches of mainspring in an unwound clock,
the time it takes, the time that's taken from it.
And I've already slammed the lift cage shut.
Are these the sacrificed?
No. They're only sleeping underground
as searchlights cross in the cloud over London
and tunnels honeycomb below in the dark
of my father's dreams. And they are the sacrificed.
And if I entered how would I . . .
Back outside I fight to catch my breath
and squeeze around, but now I'm sure I'm lost.
The tunnels fork, detour and reconnect
and circles within circles corkscrew back
to one faint star, or luminous dial of a watch
down a well, which, as I near, expands
into a thumbprint, maelstrom, weather system.
Swept up in its spiral arms, I'm dragged
down deeper, to the centre, to the freak
whose den now opens out around me –
– an airless room of baby food and wheelchairs
where the nurse arrives through muslin-filtered light
to hoover, plump, switch off *Columbo*,
and bring to the ancient bull-headed bastard its bedpan.
And when, at last, it lifts its fleshy, palsied,
toothless, half-blind, almost human head,

it's me.

        Whom did you expect? it retches
from its blackened lung, *I'm not your father,*
son. Mine is a worked-out seam whose walls
get disappeared, caved-in, carved out.
Back out of it now, before you lose your thread.
Go home, unpick the knot you've made,
leave it skitter in long waves across the tarmac
unspooled like the guts of a crushed cassette,
pay out whatever bloody yarn you must
though it wind through olive grove, ruin,
renamed road at first light where you're last seen walking,
just, to the rest of your own life, whoever you are,
and no king's daughter holding the end of your line.

A Messenger

With no less purpose than the swifts
that scrawl my name across the sky,
the hand of an obsessed pianist
quivers inches from my face.

She's anchored so she hangs mid-air
like an angel in a Christmas play.
As fidgety, but tinier, and she's forgot
her only line, *Fear not.*

With no less purpose,
than her prey, the fritillary,
flicks a wing and swells the Yangtze,
she's spun a filament across my path.

I could no more cross this line
and wreck her morning's work
than graph the plot that brought me
eye to compound eye with her.

I'd worry for her, out so far
on such tenuous connections,
but the crosshairs of the gunsight
are implied in her precision.

Quease

for P.F. *mea culpa*

Welcome to the afterlife. Or life.
I'd know that clammy pallor anywhere,
the vertigo that Chuang Tzu must have felt
who dreamt he was a butterfly, just once,
then spent a lifetime puking up his rice
because he really *was* a butterfly
now dreaming he was Chuang Tzu. Breathe.
Sailors say to look at the horizon,
the edge from which you've lately plummeted.
Trust me. I'm a connoisseur of quease.

Do you want the vomitorium?
I've fitted out an ancient Orgone Box,
although I rarely get that far myself,
and being closed in only makes it worse.
Too many bouts bareknuckled with amnesia,
I'd wake up in a cubicle in detox,
or clawing at the lining of my coffin,
or in a proper job. That kind of thing.

Quease builds a portaloo about itself,
a lift that takes one passenger, then drops.
You tell the wife you need fresh air or fags
then sprint six blocks to find a working phone
to dial your other life. It isn't home.
Now listen to the message that you leave:
before it trips your gag reflex, look down.
Someone, something, got this far tonight.
You're standing in its pizza of despair.

It all goes back to the Confessional,
the Inquisition's passport photo booth,
just room enough to kneel and stash your gum
as boozy Father Mick slid back the screen,
already wheezing with concern to hear
how many times you'd touched yourself down there.
Who's here to blame you, or forgive you, now,
for all those lies about the lies you told,
the cats you blinded and the rats you boiled?

That's why you're not feeling quite yourself,
and why I'm talking for the two of us:
your jaw's estranged by novocaine. You're stuck
halfway between the face you got from God
– like something drawn in crayon by a child –
and the one you make up as you go,
which is even worse. I know this phiz.

Halfway into jeans that aren't me,
I've caught its profile in the fitting room,
or watched its blankness settle in the pools
of the thousand tiny downstairs loos
where I knelt in Technicolor prayer.
Once it blurred across a room-sized bed
across the ceiling of a bed-sized room.
And once, it spoke. It tapped a camera plate
and whispered in the voice of Father Mick
There's no one here but you and me and God.
Say Cheese. The flash was like an angry slap.

So when you wake tomorrow wrapped in silk
inches from some mask in which you read
the corpse complexion of the urge to purge,
the pig sweat of the will to keep it down,
when you wake and try to wriggle free
into the sunlight of your adult stage,
stop. Listen for the whizz of tiny gears.
Imago that dreams our meeting here,
the sheet you're trapped in may not be your own.

Here comes the warden fiddling with the keys.
Here comes the porter with a mop and pail.
Here comes your priest and executioner,
your co-star, foil, or rude mechanical,
a noisy wind-up spider cut from tin,
Made in China on its abdomen.
You just try telling it *There's no one here.*
Feeling better? Here it comes again.
Absolvum Te [sic]. Better out than in.

Umbrage

Let them speak now
who have so long lain at our feet.
For far too long, like stricken lovers,
we have watched them sleep.

Or ignored them. Let them rise up,
freakishly tall in the level evening sun.
Let their dark voices ring in our skulls.
Let them speak, at long last, as one.

Haunts

Don't be afraid, old son, it's only me,
though not as I've appeared before,
on the battlements of your signature,
or margin of a book you can't throw out,
or darkened shop front where your face
first shocks itself into a mask of mine,
but here, alive, one Christmas long ago
when you were three, upstairs, asleep,
and haunting *me* because I conjured you
the way that child you were would cry out
waking in the dark, and when you spoke
in no child's voice but out of radio silence,
the hall clock ticking like a radar blip,
a bottle breaking faintly streets away,
you said, as I say now, *Don't be afraid.*

December 27 1999

Some Notes

The Break – Daisy and Violet Hilton were the Siamese Twins in Todd Browning's 1933 film *Freaks*.

Reprimands – In the Gospels, the name of the apostle Thomas is always accompanied by the epithet 'the twin'.

The Years – *Penetrar el espejo*, 'Penetrate the mirror', a Santeria invocation. The spirits are invited to emerge from the mirror's surface and inhabit the body of the supplicant.

The Palm – Django Reinhardt and one 'P. DeMan' stayed at the same hotel in Cannes in 1942, the Palm, where Reinhardt was playing. Louis Vola was the bassist and manager of Reinhardt's band, The Hot Club de France.

Conjure – L. *conjurare*, to swear together, a double oath.

SAFEST

A note on title and content

'Safest' is the name of the computer file in which Michael had stored the poems towards his next collection. On the day he was taken into hospital, although we had very little time before he lost consciousness, he told me that these were the poems he wanted published. I don't know whether he had intended this as the book's title (previous folders were called 'Safe' and 'Safer'), or if it was simply a way of keeping track. But 'Safest' seemed somehow appropriate, and as near as we could get to a title he'd chosen himself.

As to the manuscript, we used only the poems he had selected, resisting the temptation to put back in those he had previously rejected, or include material not yet finished. The exception to this is the fragment of a longer poem about Chief Francis O'Neill, which would I know have been in the book had he lived to complete it – it was a project dear to his heart.

Maddy Paxman
7th May 2005

But the Duende – where is the Duende? Through the empty arch enters a mental air blowing insistently over the heads of the dead, seeking new landscapes and unfamiliar accents; an air bearing the odour of child's spittle, crushed grass, and the veil of a Medusa announcing the unending baptism of all newly created things.

Lorca

Contents

– I –

– II –

– III –

– IV –

– I –

In dancing, a single step, a single movement of the body that is graceful and not forced, reveals at once the skill of the dancer. A singer who utters a single word ending in a group of four notes with a sweet cadence, and with such facility that he appears to do it quite by chance, shows with that touch alone that he can do much more than he is doing.

Castiglione, *The Book of the Courtier*

Upon A Claude Glass

A lady might pretend to fix her face,
but scan the room inside her compact mirror –

so gentlemen would scrutinize this glass
to gaze on Windermere or Rydal Water

and pick their way along the clifftop tracks
intent upon the romance in the box,

keeping unframed nature at their backs,
and some would come to grief upon the rocks.

Don't look so smug. Don't think you're any safer
as you blunder forward through your years

squinting to recall some fading pleasure,
or blinded by some private scrim of tears.

I know. My world's encircled by this prop,
though all my life I've tried to force it shut

The Whip

After Lu Chi (261–303)

Sometimes your writing's a soft tangle of subtleties
undercutting one another, blurring the paths
and you arrive at a washed-out bridge or rockslide.
Leave it. Don't try to end what's finished.
The well-aimed phrase is a whip, your poem a horse,
stamping and snorting and straining at the bit.
He wants to win as much as you do, and the whip
will serve better than a web of fine thoughts.
Just make sure you know when you've won.

I Hold in my Hand an Egg

I hold it aloft between finger and thumb
Like a quail's only smaller, unspeckled.
Be careful, you say, don't drop it.
It may be the egg of the threatened pygmy ghost owl,
and you have broken the law by removing it.

Or *Go on,* you may say, *turn it into a dart,*
or a minnow, a mainspring, a match aflame,
or make it disappear entirely
like that thought I had moments ago
before you began speaking.

Or *No,* you may say, *leave it.*
This egg is replete with meaning.
It is the egg of itself, its own egg,
the philosopher's breakfast.
And you are the Buddha.

Or you may rise and take up arms,
having recognized the egg as *hope*
and my gesture as the signal to an armed cell,
a gesture to be danced or cast in bronze one day.
And I have broken the law by performing it.

Hazards

1

Once upon a time there was a dark blue suit.
And one fine morning the chamberlain laid it out upon a bed
and the ministers of state assembled round it singing
God preserve and protect the emperor!

2

Don't worry. I gave the dancing monkey your suicide note.
Was it something important? How was I to know?
He's probably torn it to pieces by now or eaten it
or substituted every word for one adjacent in the dictionary.

3

And suddenly there came a sound from heaven as of a rushing
    mighty wind,
and cloven tongues like as of fire sat upon the heads of the
    disciples
and they began to speak with other tongues
in order to confound the multitude.

4

Was it the white pine face like a new moon?
The wet splutter and moan of the shakuhachi?
Was it the actor's dispersal in gesture and smoke?
What part of Noh did you not understand?

The apparatus

What was that exquisite name,
Could I but reach and touch it?
    The hand arranging beads across
Her cold hand in the casket.

Where is that gentle token
By which I tell my love?
    This unopened envelope,
This single empty glove.

She was my lover when we met
How could I betray her?
    The stillness in the photograph
Of a raging river.

Where are the tools by which I map
These planetary motions?
    They come and go beyond your reach.
They make their own decisions.

Who is my accuser?
Who keeps watch all afternoon?
    A glass eye, in a locked drawer,
In a forgotten room.

A Darkroom

I want to keep Klein in this red dark,
and the rawness in my nose and throat.
I want to stay apprenticed to his trade
and I require your assistance.
He's showing me his mother and five sisters
burning back from nothing, fixing them.
I want to come back to this now and again.
I want to retain Klein in the lamp's glare
at his bench, spilling tea, his twenty-minute
emphysema bark, the lung's soft whistle
through the acrid evening to closing up.
I need him to explain this process clearly,
keep him squinting through a jeweller's eyepiece
tinting and retouching faces caught in marriage.
A watchmaker's finesse: ultraviolet irises,
an undertaker's repertoire: rose cheeks
and bloody lips. And here, along his arm –
though my mother's warned me not to stare –
I need to keep them there, the numbers,
crude and blue and blurred and not consecutive,
and keep that ghost who never meets my eye,
his wife, their mad son's shaky scribbles home
in the faint grey blunted pencil they allow him,
read out, wept over, locked back in their strongbox ark,
Klein ramming a broom at the ceiling to silence
the whore who works the cops above his studio,
his sickening breath, but now *I talk too much
and now it's late, late, and your people will be worried*
and as I leave he switches on the light.
I need your help to make that sharp
before it blurs or burns itself to random
as the radio gets tuned to rapid deafening ads,
baseball scores in Spanish, or static, and the dog snarls,
the chain clatters at the door slammed shut behind me.

– II –

And it shall come to pass in the last days, saith God, I will pour out of my Spirit upon all flesh: and your sons and your daughters shall prophesy, and your young men shall see visions, and your old men shall dream dreams: And on my servants and on my handmaidens I will pour out in those days of my Spirit; and they shall prophesy: And I will shew wonders in heaven above, and signs in the earth beneath; blood, and fire, and vapour of smoke: The sun shall be turned into darkness, and the moon into blood, before the great and notable day of the Lord come.

From The Safe House

I can just see Claire your good wife reading you this.
It has arrived this morning at your orchard in Vera Cruz
where your four brown daughters hector six chickens
and you lie beneath the dusty blue pickup
tying back the exhaust with a rusty hanger,
getting ready for the long haul north.

There are parts she skips, parts about her.
And parts I've yet to write or find a way to write.
The paper she reads from is yellowed, sharp-creased,
badly typed, postmarked Chicago, decades late,
from a Reagan winter, Pax Americana for Grenada,
the coldest winter of the life of the mind.

Soon I'll climb through snowdrifts to post it
from our clapboard student commune on the South Side
on a night six mummies dug from permafrost
huddle in coats breathing clouds in a room of books,
watching the last chair leg gutter on the grate
towards the heat death of its universe.

But for now it's still flickering, and Claire is beside me.
I'm too cold to talk, too cold to think, except of her.
I hear you hammer the ice from your boots on the porch
and the door slams back and you blow in from Urbana
from over the lake, from marching with steelworkers.
You look at the fire, the bookshelves, and make the first move.

Four highlighted copies of *One Dimensional Man*,
old phone books, *Jaws*, *The Sensuous Woman* by J.
She's the first shovelled into the fire. You find it now,
hidden behind her, mimeographed, its staples gone to rust,
urgent and crumbly as this letter Claire's holding:
the Manual of the Weather Underground.

We'd been a safe house since '68 and never knew.
Did the Feds? Claire lets go my hand, takes it from you
and sniffs. Could it be any colder there?
Lit by flaring paperbacks and tequila she reads us,
like a bedtime story, the drill for evasion and escape.
I enclose it, with some photos of my son.

I have sent them you *then*, to the farm you planned,
to the heat haze in which you seem to waver,
where you lie beneath the same unsteerable wreck
your wife taught me to drive when you were drunk
and which I still own a seventh of, let's not forget,
(Tell him we never slept together, Claire)

instead of *now*, when I hear of your death,
after your stroke at my age give a month or two,
now, when you never made it to Mexico
and Claire remarried and never had children
and the clapboard safe house fell down at last
and the blue pickup went for scrap years back.

Music Sounds and Helen Passeth over the Stage

Stage direction, 'The Tragicall History of Dr. Faustus'

Fireworks crackle and the groundlings gasp and cough
and a drag queen in stiff brocade and starched ruff
glides across the stage on a starry trolley drawn by ropes.
Puppet. Hellbait. Tricktrap. Doctor, wait! She isn't real.
You're doing all the work. She has no lines –
all smoke and candlelight and burning towers.
Not that peerless dame of Greece, this poxy boy
dangling beneath a spangly sky in Rotherhithe
this thirtieth winter of Elizabeth. Curtain.

High summer. Locusts chirrup in the scrub.
Gongs. Ægypt. Enter: Athenian actor chanting
My name is Helen and I will now recount my sorrows.
The gods abducted her, she claims, and sent to Troy
an eidolon of cloud, desire, and big big trouble.
Nobody believes her but they let themselves believe,
these citizens gazing, like adulterous lovers,
through rushlight, moths and incense
toward the still eyes in the white mask.

Look up. Here she is with me up in the gods!
She came to me in tears. What could I do?
I've just been telling her, poor child, she's not to blame.
For just as the owl plummets down, talons wide for the fieldmouse,
just as the drowned are conveyed by the tides to their homes,
such are the whims of the gods and the long views of generals,
such is our nakedness helplessness innocence hubris etcetera.
And she's been pointing out the players for me
having brightened somewhat.

Angelus Novus

As in this amateur footage of a lynch mob when someone hoists a
metal folding chair and commences to batter the swinging corpse
even as others hack at its limbs with machetes, just so Achilles, his
frenzy a runaway train, yokes up his team and drags Hector's carcass
around and around like . . . Stop. Rewind.

Hector dying on his knees in the dust whispering *Prove you're a
man, then, swear by your soul, swear by your gods you won't feed
my corpse to your dogs.*

Fuck you spits Achilles. Freeze frame. Mid-blink, Hector looks into
Achilles' eyes and takes all the time in the world to recall his last
embrace of Andromache and, it hardly now surprises him, to look
back at the future advancing behind him, to his own father
kissing the hands of this killer, the monster taking Priam's hand and
weeping with him, the sound of their sobbing filling the camp. Play
on. Hector's face slams to the dust.

Try to look at this: blind flash victims. Nagasaki. In their endless
1945 they face the camera as unaware of the photographer as they
are of you, viewer. Just so, rage-blind Achilles cannot now glimpse in
Hector's eyes, just before they empty, the terrible pity.

Guilt Wasn't Why She Was Weeping

Like the searchlights that glare through the nursery's breathmisted window,
like the static that rasps through the speakers submerging the warning,
like the heat haze of summer that ripples the level horizon,
just so did Helen
take silvery veils on her shoulders.

And she walked the wall weeping where Priam was eyeing up targets.
Then, like a warrior taking his fieldglasses, softly
Priam called out to her, Helen, come sit with me, daughter
kissing her tears away
whispering, Child, don't take on so.

But she threw off his hand – guilt wasn't why she was weeping –
and that whisper she answered with flashed like a silvery spearpoint,
like the static that rasps through the speakers submerging the warning,
like the heat haze of summer
that ripples the level horizon.

Disquietude

Would you know it if our phone was tapped?
Would you hear a series of clicks, for example?
Or the sound of breathing? Or policemen typing?
After the next caller hangs up stay on the line.
Stay on until you're sure.

One day when we were younger and hornier
I stashed a tape recorder underneath our bed. Please don't be angry.
I wanted to keep the noises we were when we weren't ourselves,
but all the mic picked up was wheezing springs. Just as well.
It would be like listening to strangers now.

Our names have sounds besides the ones we hear.
Sometimes, when I wake beside you in the night
and the door of sleep slams shut and locks behind me,
I hear it creep up out of silence, a brash hush,
a crowded emptiness, the static of the spheres.

It's like a tap left on. But it's my own warm blood,
the flood that's washing all the names away,
of schoolmates, kings, the principal export of somewhere,
and all the sounds as well – a lullaby, a child's voice –
my own warm blood that must be blessed.

No recording devices are allowed in this hall.
The lights dim, and onstage they're coughing,
turning pages, giving the score their indivisible attentions,
getting settled for the next movement
which features no one and is silent.

The Moko

Muscles of silence are rolling miles offshore at night,
and each an unpraised perfect wave
cresting this morning in this half-curtained room.
Nothing so dear as these should be so lost.
As any change in the true wind
will show its fingerprint in the sea,
a fresh train of ripples or waves will run
a web over waves caused by the true wind.
Singing. Log drumming. Steering roughly
north by stern bearings of the Southern Cross –
the islands are high and the clouds hover over them.
Nothing so dear as these should be forgotten.
Look on these faces tattooed with maelstroms,
branching fern fronds, with the wave's own codes.
Look on these faces and remember the webbed
imponderables of whirls and eddies.
Observe the cheek spirals – doubly inscribed
tracking the Sun inward to the centre,
the solstice, where it turns and edges
toward the Equinoctial bridge of the nose,
then on to the opposite side of the face.
Moonrise. Watch as a face turns leeward,
for any change in the true wind
will show its fingerprint in the sea.
They knew the stars and steered by singing them
and when the stars were dark, by wind,
and when the winds died, by wave swell,
bird flight, swirled shoals of luminous algae,
by phosphorescence a fathom under the outrigger.
By the million dust motes whorled in the sun shaft,
by every word adrift we whisper in this bed,
they might have sung where we've no skill to reckon.
And nothing of this could have been foreseen.
And nothing so dear as this should be forsaken.

– III –

Norton's Manner

Norton could swallow a number of half-grown frogs and bring them up alive. I remember his anxiety on one occasion when returning to his dressing-room; it seems he had lost a frog – at least he could not account for the entire flock – and he looked very much scared, probably at the uncertainty as to whether or not he had to digest a live frog. At these October Fests I saw a number of frog-swallowers, and to me they were very repulsive indeed. In fact, Norton was the only one I ever saw who presented his act in a dignified manner.

Harry Houdini

Poem On The Underground

Sirs, as ancient maps imagine monsters
so London's first anatomical charts
displayed the innards of a vast loud animal;
writhing discrete circulatory systems
venous, arterial, lymphatic, rendered
into District, Piccadilly, Bakerloo . . .
But Harry Beck's map was a circuit diagram
of coloured wires soldered at the stations.
It showed us all we needed then to know,
and knew already, that the city's
an angular appliance of intentions, not
the blood and guts of everything that happens.
Commuters found it 'easier to read'.

My new 3D design improves on Beck,
restoring something of the earlier complexity.
See, here I've drawn the ordinary lines
but crossing these, weaving through the tunnels,
coded beyond the visible spectrum, I've graphed
the vector of today's security alert
due to a suspect package at Victoria,
to the person under a train at Mill Hill East,
with all the circumstantial stops between.

So the vomiting temp in the last train out of Brixton
links to the fingerless busker doing card tricks
making himself invisible to a crowded carriage.
The lines along the third dimension indicate
connections through time: here, the King's Cross fire
leads back to wartime bivouacs on station platforms
and further still, to children singing on a sunlit hill.
Admittedly my design is less accessible than Beck's,
being infinite and imperceptible, but I'm confident,
that given time, the public would embrace it.
I strongly urge the panel to consider my proposal.
Respectfully submitted, May 9, 2003.

Fragment

Irish Folk Music: A Fascinating Hobby,
With Some Account of Related Subjects,
by Police Chief Francis O'Neill, Chicago, 1910

Any change in the true wind
will show its fingerprint in the sea.
A fresh train of ripples or waves will run
a web over waves caused by the true wind.

I am the foam on the wave
I am the bright wave on the white sand
I am a foredeck gorilla
I am a lost shoe at a crossroads dance,
if anyone asks. *Still,* you may enquire,
with so few natural attributes,
why did he not stay on land?

After our rescue rations were necessarily limited almost to
starvation. One of the Kanakas had a fine flute, on which he
played a simple one-strain hymn with conscious pride
almost every evening.
Steering roughly
north by stern bearings of the Southern Cross –
the islands are high and the clouds hover over them.
They knew the stars and steered by singing them
and when the stars were dark
they steered by wind and when the winds died
they read by the wave swell, by the birdflight,
by the phosphorescence a fathom under.
They were like children.

Of course, this chance to show what could be done on the
instrument was not to be overlooked.
I am a stag for swiftness, says the chief
I am a fort for shelter
I am a remedy for flatulence. 'Tell her
I am' the true wind.
I am a loyal servant
of the Democratic administration of this city.
I am a pocket watch.

The result was most gratifying . . . My dusky brother musician
cheerfully shared his 'poi' and canned salmon with me
thereafter. When we arrived at Honolulu . . . after a voyage of
thirty-four days, all but three of the castaways were sent to
the Marine Hospital. I was one of the robust ones thanks to
my musical friend

  Its eyelid opens
and he snaps it shut.
Who are you, chief, between the tick
and tock?

I am a castaway by the albatross
I am a cracked skull in Odessa
I am a river on fire
I am innocent of all these charges.

  if anyone asks
He tells the barman,
I'm not here.

'ASSASSIN OF PRESIDENT McKINLEY AN ANARCHIST.
CONFESSES TO HAVING BEEN INCITED BY EMMA
GOLDMAN. WOMAN ANARCHIST WANTED.'

Grimoire

An intervening object does not impede the vision of the blessed . . .
Christ could see the face of his mother when she was prostrate on the
ground . . . as if he were looking directly at her face. It is clear that
the blessed can see the front of an object from the back, the face
through the back of the head.

Bartholomew Rimbertinus
On the Sensible Delights of Heaven, Venice, 1498

1

An afterlife in the theatre: 'And this, gentlemen (removes top of
skull), is the principal sulcus of the dorsolateral prefrontal cortex,
which manifests remarkable accord amongst the senses, even in the
sane. The smelling salts for Mr Bohman, Sister.'

2

To speak aloud among the sober of the sweet reek of bright green,
the soft hiss of yellow, the bitter shapes of the sound of the space in
which we speak, their lavender numbers tasting of sesame, is
indiscreet. Make sense. But only one sense at a time. To remark on
the silence breaking on the facets of a word the way light breaks
across an oilslick to the polyphonic iridescence of simultaneous
orgasm betrays one to the panicked guest whose eyes alert the host
across the room. Patience, children. Learn to hush your wonder.

3

Same again? Our hostess is engaged. She's grinding crystals finely on 'his jet shewstone' having borrowed overnight from the museum that black Aztec mirror John Dee used to talk to angels in their own tongue. She likes a bit of fun.

Someone's pounding on the door but she's caught her own gaze mid-sniff and is snagged in the talons of Quetzalcoatl, the feathered reptile trapped in the obsidian, twin god of self-reflection. She keeps to her knees as he tells her all she needs to know.

4

Keep up! The argument has run ahead, like an angry bearded black-robed bishop who leads us through a labyrinth of alleys to Chloras, goldsmith, busy through the night in his workshop of important toys. Here, a monk that kneels at clockwork prayer, here, a lady flautist trills and winks, and here, his masterpiece, that dragonfly of tin coil, springs and vermicelli gold. It tilts its head, it whirrs, it clicks its wings and – truly this the demon's work – it speaks: *Keep up! Reach out! Your day will come, Your fingers brush a face across the sea.*

5

At the commandment of the conjuror he dooth take awaie the sight
of anie one. He is a great prince, taking the forme of a thrush, except
he be brought to a chaulk triangle and therein he teacheth divinetie,
rhetorike, logike, pyromancie. He giveth men the understanding of
all birds, of the lowing of bullocks, and barking of dogs, and also of
the sound and noise of waters, he ruleth now thirtie legions of divels
who was of the celestiall orders and will possess agayne and rule the
world.

6

Keep up. The argument will run ahead outstripping words, will tear
down neural paths branching, sundering, recombining, out of sight
and far beyond your power to direct. Upgraded man, inhaling
sunlight, who listens in silence, who sees in the dark, what you might
tell us of the world beyond speech no one, no, not even you, can say.

– IV –

*I slipped from my saddle in a dark courtyard
leaving my horse to the silent grooms*

Italo Calvino

Midriver

– and is a bridge: Now to either then:
child to lolly: spark across the wire:
lover to the target of desire:
Lambeth to Westminster: back again.
Verb's a vector not a monument,
but someone skipped a stone across this river
fixing its trajectory forever
in seven arches after the event
– so stops halfway and, neither there nor there,
but cold and rained on and intransitive,
watches London switch from *when* to *where*,
why to silence in the traffic jam,
thinks I can see the borough where I live
but here is temporarily who I am.

The River Glideth Of His Own Sweet Will

Who's this buck of eighteen come up the stairs
squinting from his *Rough Guide*
across the Thames into the late June sun
towards Lambeth, the wheel, the aquarium,

and St Thomas' Hospital where you lie
in the eighth-floor intensive-care unit
wired up to a heart monitor
staring north to Big Ben's crackled face?

But now the nurse pulls shut the blinds –
not that you'd have clocked one another.
What unaided eyes could possibly connect
thirty years across Westminster bridge
through traffic fumes, crowds,
children, career, marriage, mortgage?

Southwesternmost

I've a pocketwatch for telling space,
a compass tooled for reckoning by time,
to search this quadrant between six and nine
for traces of her song, her scent, her face.
Come night, that we might seek her there, come soon,
come shade the southwest quarter of this chart,
the damaged chamber of my mother's heart.

Mare Serenitatis on the moon,
this blindspot, tearhaze, cinder in the eye,
this cloudy star when I look left and down,
this corner of the crest without a crown,
this treeless plain where she went home to die.
I almost hear it now and hold its shape,
the famine song she's humming in my sleep.

Akhmatova Variations

No, he'd never leave us here alone.
He merely became an ear of grain,
the fine rain he sang into lines,
the shine struck from wet sand at low tide,
the bedside glass of water rippling,
the eye of a horse between two blinks,
or so we think, to console ourselves.
Hear that thunderous whisper?
It's time-lapse flowers bursting from the earth.
Years pass. At last, the echo fades
and the grasses kneel to a soundless wind
we insist on hearing as a prayer
shared by sisters of a silent order,
or those humblest of words, our names.

2

Where will I find you? Among the living
or pressed between my palms in prayer,
a shade swept like a leaf among shades?
I hereby dedicate to you the following:
First, my days, entire, and the delirious dawn
when the door of sleep clicks shut behind me,
the blue fire of my eyes, open, focused,
but still twitching like a dreamer's.
And all these too I offer up:
my unblemished sacrificial flock,
blank pages in a notebook in a locked drawer,
though no God could know me as well as you,
not my interrogator, not my torturer,
not even those who took, and forgot, my kiss.

3

If only you knew what trifles spark a poem.
A scream from the flat above
and you go cold hoping it's laughter.
That chill can kick-start the engine.
Or when you hang up and I hear clicks,
or clock the car drawn up beneath my window,
the punch in my chest is the muse touching my heart.
It's brazen, this art. A poet might clench her eyes,
might stand with her face to the wall, listening
for footsteps in the corridor, trying not to think,
and suddenly a line betrays itself.

4

Two lovers walk abroad, night-riddled and bereaved
because, years hence, some perfect stranger dreams they do
and dreams their every word of parting
but can't decide the colour of his eyes,
can't aim the loaded pistol of her gaze.
They walk the darkest alleyways because
their only freedom's in obscurity
(but tell me, is that stranger you or me?).

Now deep inside the dream the moon emerges
exposing us, and now our footsteps click
into their positions on a mandala.
My whisper is a tile in a mosaic,
the sky a spray of one-star constellations:
the pupil, the tear, the full stop.

5

As we sat in deathwatch on our love,
the wraith of our first days knocked on the door,
then forced it down. There spread the silver willow
in all its splendour ghosting over us.
How could we meet its gaze or bear to suffer
the birdsong bursting from its branches,
the song of how we'd die for one another?

Not grenadiers bleeding but your night bus leaving
Not falcons and gyres but discarded desires
Not the death of the tsar but the smell of fresh tar
Not theories of language but gunplay in marriage
Not the marble of wrath but your hair in my mouth

The New Grey

It's black, it says here, but not jet, not shiny,
more the charcoal-black old family snapshots burn,
the dark of the cathedral vault aswarm with pigeons
muted to an expensive almost-blue-black.
See a woman in black? See me touching her shoulder?
We weren't friends, but . . . But what? Hear my words
blow out like lamps in series down a mine shaft?
The colour of the coal dust rising up to gag me
is this new shade, exactly. Can we discuss this?
I need to get fluent in grey if I want to survive.
I need a job to earn enough to buy that shirt
in the same unsayable shade that hid in the wardrobe
in a room I woke in as a child.

The Swear Box

They open, at forty, cabinets their fathers locked,
boys again, whispering bad words beneath blankets,
girls spitting the big verbs at their mirrors.
Something sharp and rusty on their tongues again,
something more he'd hoped to spare them:
new bedside silences for visiting hours,
new definitions for never, for over.
quiet words boomed from pulpit mics,
and, afterwards, the whispers of dark-suited cousins.
Women hugging pregnant friends practice
new phrases, concealing the chill. Grown men
yank shut the curtains of their brilliant studies
to stop the black glass listening.

A Sicilian Defence

It is another story altogether
by lanternlight, beneath two birches
and the sound of a shallow river
where two men are playing chess
for as long as either will remember,
opening P–K4, P–QB4.
It's not a question of either/or –
one might be my father, or me at sixty.
The other might as well be me
thinking: his right's my left, my left
his right. I see it now in a different light.
I know it now by another name.

Is it any wonder then this game
runs on through this and every night
forever, lit by lanternlight, two birches
and the sound of a river?

Exile's End

You will do the very last thing.
Wait then for a noise in the chest,
between depth charge and gong,
like the seadoors slamming on the car deck.
Wait for the white noise and then cold astern.

Gaze down over the rim of the enormous lamp.
Observe the skilled frenzy of the physicians,
a nurse's bald patch, blood. These will blur,
as sure as you've forgotten the voices
of your childhood friends, or your toys.

Or, you may note with mild surprise,
your name. For the face they now cover
is a stranger's and it always has been.
Turn away. We commend you to the light,
Where all reliable accounts conclude.

Two Spells For Sleeping

Eight white stones
in a moonlit garden,
to carry her safe
across the bracken
on a gravel path
like a silvery ribbon
seven eels in the urge of water
a necklace in rhyme
to help her remember
a river to carry her
unheard laughter
to light about her
weary mirror
six candles for a king's daughter
five sighs for a drooping head
a prayer to be whispered
a book to be read
four ghosts to gentle her bed
three owls in the dusk falling
what is that name
you hear them calling?
In the soft dark welling,
two tales to be telling,
one spell for sleeping,
one for kissing,
for leaving.

UNCOLLECTED POEMS

Contents

No

"I gave up being serious about making pictures around the time I made a film with Greer Garson and she took a hundred and twenty-five takes to say no."

– Robert Mitchum

I want to go back and finish my degree.
Give me back my carrel in the library
in the basement, under that strobing striplight.
I want to wear the same suit for six years,
develop an amphetamine psychosis
and sit before Paul DeMan with two ideas
inked on my knuckles.
I want to vomit pure sherry
an hour into the department sherry hour.

Change the title and the leading lady.
Keep the dialogue. The ideas wash off.

Fin

When you stand half out of your lives,
half into your coats, half-heartedly
reading the foot-high radiant names
as they slip up and out of your minds,
watch for mine, misspelled
among the best boys, dolly grips,
clapper loaders, animal trainers,
Ms Basinger's dialect coach,
the ushers, the ghost-lit ice cream lady,
and the man with the uncontrollable cough.

That's me, straight out of central casting,
the hero of the prequel to my biopic
(some has-been) IS *The Man Who Never Was*
[not the re-make, postmod with air-quotes
but a re-mix, scooped out in air-brackets]
Mighty in *The Citizen Cain*
Mutiny, *Feisty* in *Snow White and the Seven*
Samurai. Now, for the first time,
Weary, lip-synched, but "as himself",

You'll see. You'll stand for years. The credits only end
when you see yourself ("special thanks to") scroll by,
slip the capstans, and flap on the reel
like a sound effect. For *The Birds*.

Windy Chrysanthemums

How irritating!
The way you twitch your fingers
when I read my poems.

I wonder if you
wouldn't mind not doing that.
It's irritating.

Fifteen syllables!
This middle line has seven.
The others have five.

Would you like a drink?
Let me recommend this one.
I've hardly touched it.

Cicadas

Only one, and then many,
scissoring through the summer dusk,
neither calling nor answering but singing
all risen from the earth, from years
of inexplicable darkness, from dust,
all having laboured toward the sun
out of the dry carapace clinging,
all gone at last among the leaves
to make music into the evening.

And nothing,
not the great cellist in the hall,
not the sound of the Intercity
bearing down at you on the level crossing,
no, not even your name
or a sound you thought might be your name
gasped out by your lover
safe in your arms a final time,
can rise like this, or fall away so swiftly.

In An Unsigned Yearbook

If a year is a prayer you're to get by heart,
It's far and away too long.
If its days are a rhyme for remembering,
the words you heard were wrong.
If it were a song you were meant to sing,
It wouldn't be this song. Whereas,
If it's a book in which you read
And are read yourself in turn
(A big book, say, an expensive book,
In some language you suffer to learn),
The infinite shift of gist within gist
Would make these pages burn. Not that they will,
Not now, nor at year's end, not after, nor until.

Kaleidoscope

Marina Warner wakes me in the lay-by
I pulled into at dawn when I blinked
awake on the A road doing 60. Marina,
or someone like her, is arguing
with Susan Sontag about media and libido,
mermaids and Madonna. It's 4PM,
Dorset. Grey rainlight and a reek of silage.

I slap my legs awake and crawl outside to find
I'm parked by Teddy's Friendly Pig and Poultry Farm,
and Teddy's got Radio 4 rasping loud as an air raid
through tinny speakers rigged above the sties.
I need a phone, coffee, and a toilet so
I pay my 50p and stagger in.
The hairy piglets try to eat my shoes
as Marina drowns in static, then Techno-something
whumping as I ring you and it rings and rings.

Where are you? For all you know I might be
halfway through the windscreen in a ditch.
I see you opening the door to the police,
fainting in the hallway, sobbing in black
as you sort my souvenirs and letters.
(How would they reconstruct my life, I wonder,
who never kept a diary? Last year I tried
collating the summers, the lovers, the songs,
But 1975 was missing, and part of '77)
And now you're smiling, healing, forgetting,
a surface closing smooth above me.

I zip my jacket as it starts to rain.
Big drops pock the dust, sending hens screeching
as a rush of interference swamps the DJ
and I hunker in the incubator shed, shivering,
suddenly ghostlier than these frequencies,
than the signals raining through the tin walls,
through my body and yours and my hand is shaking
as I punch your number but I can't hear above the noise
because the girl in the office is twirling the dial,
strafing the farm with random chords and syllables.

I want to kill her but her T-shirt says GIVE UP.
Instead, I smile. She doesn't. "I wonder," I yell,
"what do they like to listen to, the chickens?"
"Nothing," she says, "but it scares away the foxes."
Gone to earth, I think, slamming the car door,
and I make for home beneath the storm, driving
slow, like a fugitive, a mourner, a learner.

Rite for Bill

Forever, throughever,
this morning by screenlight,
by tonguelight, by fleshlight
braided through the moment
of this his death
by striplight flickering out
between our words, our rite
unwhispered, the mist breathed
back to mere breath,
the breath sucked
back to first cry
first wet gasp back,
to the liquid pulse, to the still,
still we'll remember this morning,
we say, forever, by-
-ever, forever, whoever
we are, or were, and will.

Blinder

He is standing in the shadow of the sun.
At the commandement of the conjuror he dooth
take awaie the sight of anie one.
He is a great prince, taking the forme of a thrush,
He made the market. He makes it crash.

And he is big. Oh, he is global,
He is negatives of the earth as seen from space.
He is hungry, adaptable, has a stake in your success.
He sleeps in the deepest part of sleep
and has already read and censored this.

He is a bright foam on the wave,
sustained cold fusion in a plasma cocoon,
an incurable virus, a pocket watch.
His eyelid opens and he snaps it shut.
He casts a cold eye. He eyes you up.

Sharks Asleep

That the bar fell to a hush to hear her sing,
That oilslick sheen of feathers on a blackbird's wing,
That everything is what it is and no other thing,

Should not detain us overlong, who like sharks have found
A current surging in the deep where our sleep is sound.
Glasses clink. Voices rise. The song is drowned.

Darkness and the Subject

The basic requirement of darkness
is that it enables us to extinguish the shape
of an object.

A girl beneath a tree, for example,
with the night behind her,
can only be forgotten by her absence

of outline, and
as the direction of darkness changed,
it would reveal less and less of the tree.

In this way we can select
and use darkness to reveal
or subdue qualities in a subject.

Ex Libris

They sleep somewhere in darkness and damp rot.
Brown, out of print, and flaking into dust.
Of the instruments of our enlightenment

– dry icicles plunged in the base of the skull,
drunken kisses after closing time,
the hours, days, the years –

all that remains is a phrase, a rhyme,
a reflex whispered on the lips and tongue
like the final blue white gasp of the gas mantle
which is, *mutatis mutandis*,
all that remains of our enlightenment.

Gimmick

Imagine an ankle length blue leather coat. Imagine it strutting down an alley on its own. Now slip inside the coat a young Italian American male sporting a Zapata moustache, shoulder length hair, green and yellow platform shoes. You have assembled my memory of Gimmick in 1975. Wait. Put this length of chain in his pocket. Put this blotter sheet of acid in his wallet.

Gimmick is getting in stock for this term's business and he wants my help acquiring some speed from a none too fastidious local physician. He's not convincingly overweight himself but I can tip the scales with a little help from the ashtrays, aquarium gravel and fishing weights Gimmick's stuffing into my pockets and down the pair of ill fitting cowboy boots he's lent me for the afternoon. "Just weigh in and take the pills." In payment for my help I can keep a third of the speed and the boots.

I wait while Gimmick sits on his waterbed, poised with a waist high two handled bong beneath a DayGlo Jimi Hendrix poster. He's in a meeting, offering a franchise to two young Black men, Jimmy and Cootchie, who look a bit twitchy. Gimmick is talking security. "You can't just walk around the projects on your own." He's just taken a manly hit and he's keeping back a lungful as he croaks, "You guys gotta get yourselves a big nigger." He exhales a roomful of smoke. Me, I've never heard a White guy throw that word in a Black guy's face without big trouble. I'm tensed for the Big Ugly but Jimmy and Cootchie astonish me. "We got one."

I've upset Gimmick. He thinks I'm ripping him off. He's grabbed my collar and pulled my face up to his fist. But his voice is almost breaking. There are tears in his eyes.

A member of the "savage skulls", a local gang, has been shot by the police. Small wonder. The skulls have been working hard to outdo all their rivals in terror. But last month they crossed the line. Gimmick's cousin Tony had foolishly joined and then attempted to quit the skulls, and for this insult they killed him. They bound him hand and foot and threw him in a room with a dog they'd specially starved for this.

Habit

(Lyrics for a film by Miranda Pennell)

Elizabeth Pickett
died December 12th 1789 age 23 yrs
in Confequence of her Cloathes Taking Fire the Previous Evening.

Mother, forgive me, I'm not in the habit of writing.
I write to tell you I am much distressed.
"Habit allows the subject to disregard irrelevant stimuli"
And every habit must be starched
And every nylon ballgown pressed.
Fold over. Spray. Iron along the pleat.
      Unfold. Repeat.

I write to tell you that I've had no peace
      since I was eight and played at fancy dress
since I was very small and played with shades.
Faces in paisley. Wallpaper faces.
      Net curtains lifting and whispering. Oh,
not since I played in our house's darkest places.

See what's on the other side
you'd say. Interference. Ghosts.
Trying to touch you again and again
like a child grabbing at pictures in a book,
      net curtains lifting and whispering,
trying to explain,
I have to turn the doorknob
three times fast, spin clockwise,
I have to touch my fingers to my lips.
I only have to breathe to say your name.

In the rooms of the house in my head
the shades I see
are not just the shades of the dead,
who bear no allegiance to this earth,
and of the dead not just their selves –
Phantom pregnancy. Phantom birth.
Phantom laundry – unfold.
        Repeat – I write to tell you

I write to tell you, though I have no time to write,
though ashes lift and flutter on my breath,
        when I was eight and played in fancy dress,
and whoever she was she is wearing my mind.
Elizabeth,
dressing in my skin,
as an eager young girl in a crinoline,
for a dance in the middle of winter.

The moth mistakes the candle for the moon
by which it navigates. It overcompensates.
It spirals in and burns.
Lucky the child who watches this and learns.
        Repeat.
Three ways to keep my writing table neat:
Before I write I spin round clockwise,
twist the doorknob,
touch my fingers to my lips.
        Unfold. Repeat. I cannot keep
these creases straight.
And maybe that last long night in December
when she'd lit every lamp in the house
and she stood at the top of the stairs,
I remember, the fiddlers playing
the Dashing White Sergeant
for the dance of the last long night of her life,
her sleeve took light.

Am I such thoughts
or something that thinks them?
Forgive me. I'm giddy. I'm alone. I'm afraid
as I'm not in the habit of writing
I'm not in the habit of folding the paper three times
to fit in the envelope. I can't lick the stamp.
It appears I'm enveloped in flame. I'm afraid
that this simply won't do, Elizabeth.

And her name in my head is a stone in my shoe.
    (God knows where that stone belongs.)

And her grave is a rhyme for remembering,
    (but the words I read were wrong).

And her death is a dance I'm to get by heart,
    (but it's far and away too long).

And I have to wrestle her day after day,
    (but mother, she's too strong).

And if she were a song I were meant to sing,
    I wouldn't sing this song.

Two alternative Westminster Bridge sonnets

Vacancy

Earth hasn't anything to show more fair,
so pay attention. Flick back the curtains,
slip back the duvet, contemplate my nakedness,
my open mouth, the precincts of my temple.
Still time to study my exquisite indifference,
my eyeballs twitching beneath the lids
in rapid variations indecipherable
as an ascending diver's spume of bubbles.
This is the beauty spot, the gentle sniper's nest,
the view from the bridge between sleeping and waking,
and this is your moment to play the immortal.
An hour from now I'll be occupied. Occupied?
Hell, roads will be jammed across the capital.
Ringtones, Drivetime, A–Zs. Wakey Wakey.

Watch

Morning on the bridge between the worlds.
I'm half awake and watching you asleep.

Your lips are open and your fist uncurls
as if in offering. I'd give my life to keep
that gift, who cannot shield you from my death,
and keep this vigil lightly though I know
I'm losing you with every mortal breath.

And suddenly I'm drunk with vertigo
having glimpsed the landscape from this height:
School yards, hospitals and factories lie
unprotected in that naive light
stretching toward a distant darker sky
and fading in the haze of every mile.
The day is cool and bright. You wake and smile.

Ogata

The longest day ends
And puts its children to bed
They believe our lies.

Still asleep at dawn,
A blizzard in a garden
In a far city.

Bright clouds of glass dust
Billow from shot-out mirrors,
Lady from Shanghai.

You slept with my wife?
Someday we'll laugh about it.
The moon in the pines.

B Side Vocal

Oh ashes to ashes
And dust to dust
If God doesn't save me
You women must.
If you hang up,
The walls close in.
So let's live together
    In venial sin

From dawn to dusk
And dusk to dawn
You're the vaguest woman
Ever been born
If you don't want my baguette
Keep out of my bin.
Wake me when you're ready
    For a venial sin.

Now I keep a record
Of who you've been dating.
And I keep phoning
But I get call waiting.
I keep on knocking, lover,
But you still won't let me in
And I got a subpoena
    For a venial sin

Oh tell me how long
how long must I wait
You'd make a china panda
Masturbate.
You got a balloon.
I got a pin.
Let's go down in flames
    Of venial sin

Oh Life is short.
And Death is tall.
I saw him loitering
in your downstairs hall.
He'd a list of addresses
Where they never let him in
And every one was marked with v
For "venial sin"

Life's too short. Death's too tall.
This song's too long
And your flat's too small.
There's mouse shit
In the muesli
And the walls are too thin
For the audible expression
Of venial sin

So pack up your bags,
Get your vague ass on the bus
Pack enough of yourself
For the two of us.
Press the bottom buzzer,
I'll come down and let you in
And before you touch those carrier bags
We'll get stuck in.

Oh ashes to ashes
And dust to dust
If God doesn't save me
You women must.
If you hang up,
The walls close in.
So let's live together
In venial sin

Fugue

A helicopter circles your estate.
It thumps like the heart of a man on fire
so the boys on the stairs thumb the bass higher.
Your windows vibrate
to a code you're not supposed to crack
like the carrier signal the woofers send,
like birdsong, but the bottom end,
like the canon that makes the cradle rock
that you heard long ago on a harpsichord track,
the distant shelling on Landowska's Bach –
thudding in mud, and beyond, the order
of figure surrendering to ground
that thrummed the warm soup all around
for months in your mother.
Now there isn't any sound. Listen.
All they came to say must have got said.
As we've been whispering in your room
the boys above went home. The slugs resumed.
The clothespegs roost above your flower bed.

Veritas

A boy is licking a lamppost in December
He will stand here stuck forever
squinting left and right for his friends.
Moses with his mouthful of ember.

Centuries old, he has learned its taste.
Silenced by his thirty foot steel stammer,
he dared. And became his own monument.
Surely his tea is ready.

All around the boy great flakes drift down
taking their time on the way to the pavement
A boy is licking a lamppost in December.
His mother is going to kill him.

Acknowledgements

Shibboleth

Acknowledgement is gratefully made to the editors of the following periodicals, in which poems appeared: *Poetry Review, Poetry (Chicago), The Massachusetts Review, The Mississippi Review, The Chicago Review, Kansas Quarterly, Seneca Review, Orbis*.

'Machines' appeared as a limited edition designed by Barbara Tetenbaum, published by Circle Press Publications. 'Smith' appeared as a limited edition, also designed by Barbara Tetenbaum, and published by Triangular Press. 'Cadenza' was broadcast on *Poetry Now* (BBC Radio 3). 'Shibboleth' was also broadcast and appeared in pamphlet form as part of the 1987 National Poetry competition.

The quotation from Son House in 'Interviews' comes from Stefan Grossman's *Delta Blues Guitar*, Oak Publications, 1969.

Shibboleth replaces *Slivers* (Thompson Hill, Chicago, 1985) and includes revised versions of some of the poems in that collection.

Errata

Acknowledgements are gratefully made to the Arts Council of Great Britain, and to the editors of the following anthologies and periodicals in which some of these poems have appeared: the *Sunday Times, Poetry (Chicago)*, the *New Yorker*, the *New Statesman, Poetry Review*, the *Times Literary Supplement, The Honest Ulsterman, Verse, The Jacaranda Review, The Poetry Book Society Anthology 1991–1992*.

'Liverpool' was commissioned for BBC Radio's *Kaleidoscope* programme.

Several of the poems were first published by the Silver Buckle Press, University of Wisconsin–Madison Libraries, in a limited edition chapbook, *O'Ryan's Belt*.

Conjure

Thanks to the editors of the following magazines, in which some of these poems appeared: *Epoch*, the *Guardian*, the *Independent*, *Metre*, the *New Yorker*, the *New York Times*, the *Observer*, *Poetry (Chicago)*, *Poetry Review*, the *Sunday Times*, the *TLS*, *Verse*.

And many thanks to The Arts Council of England, the Harold Hyam Wingate Foundation, and the Ingram Merrill Foundation (US).

Index of titles

Index of first lines